SUPPORTING STUDENT EXECUTIVE FUNCTIONS

SUPPORTING STUDENT EXECUTIVE FUNCTIONS

Insights and Strategies for Educators

LISA CAREY and ALEXIS REID

CAST | Until learning has no limits·

© 2024 CAST, Inc.

All rights reserved. No part of this publication may be reproduced, stored in a retrieval system, or transmitted in any form or by any means, electronic, mechanical, photocopying, recording, or otherwise, without the prior permission of the Publisher.

ISBN (paperback): 978-1-943085-18-7
ISBN (ebook): 978-1-943085-19-4

Library of Congress Control Number: 2023944675

Cover and interior design by Happenstance Type-O-Rama
All images included courtesy of the authors except where noted.

Published by CAST Professional Publishing,
an imprint of CAST, Inc.,
Lynnfield, Massachusetts, USA

For information about special discounts for bulk purchases, please email *publishing@cast.org* or visit *publishing.cast.org*.

To my dad, who taught me about inclusion through his actions. To my mom, who taught me the importance of teaching well. To my (much cooler) sister, for providing me with endless stories of how two sisters can think and learn in very different but equally effective ways. To my husband, for supporting and pushing me to use my talents. And to our son, for being my hype-man.

—LISA CAREY

My work to support the understanding and development of executive functioning is dedicated to all the students in my life and around the world who have been misunderstood. Throughout my life I have witnessed many learners, of all ages and backgrounds, experience everyday struggles to activate their executive functioning skills despite the intellect, motivation, and desire to do well. When we recognize, embrace, and support variability in executive functioning across the life span, we can strategically approach how individuals learn, grow, and find their purpose in life. This is for you all.

This book is also dedicated to those who continually show up and support all that I do. My parents and my brother continue to be beacons of light for me—especially my mother, who has always guided us to live purposeful lives through the fullest expressions of who we are. I am inspired by and grateful for those closest to me—my family, colleagues, friends, and mentors—and your presence, guidance, and love are felt and appreciated.

—ALEXIS REID

Contents

Welcome! . . . . *ix*
Introduction *1*

Part I: Understanding Executive Functioning

  1 Signs of Struggle 11
  2 What Are Executive Functions? 23
  3 Executive Functions and the Developing Brain 33
  4 Executive Functioning and Universal Design for Learning . . . 47

Part II: Developing and Supporting Executive Functioning

  5 Establishing Clear Goals 61
  6 Determining Priorities and Creating a Plan 79
  7 Teaching Metacognition and Reflection 97
  8 Mindfully Designing a Learning Environment to Support Executive Functioning 113
  9 Scaffolding Learning With Agendas, Transitions, Routines, and Breaks 129
  10 Using Mindfulness, Movement, and the Arts to Support Executive Functions 151

Final Thoughts *161*
References *165*
Notes From the Authors *169*
Acknowledgments *177*
Index *179*
About the Authors *189*

Welcome!

Thanks for picking up this book from CAST Publishing. While you might expect a book from CAST to focus on the guiding principles of UDL and all of the UDL Guidelines, this book will not. Instead, we'll focus on one UDL Guideline in particular: Provide options to support executive functions. If you're looking for a book focused on UDL in its entirety, CAST has some *really* great options; this just isn't one of them. But if you've wondered what executive functions are, what they have to do with learning, or how you can build a learning environment that better supports and develops these critical skills, you're in the right place.

Introduction

Lisa was in her eighth year of teaching when she received her first professional training about executive functions. The subject wasn't part of the regular teacher education coursework, nor had it been part of any professional development provided at any of the three schools where she'd worked. Rather, this introduction to the concept of executive functions and their relationship to teaching and learning was offered at a daylong workshop by a parents' group. Lisa remembers, "The whole day was one big 'aha!' moment. Finally, I had a term and way to frame how and why my students were struggling academically even when I knew that *they knew* the content." She'd heard the term *executive functions* before. She'd seen them in the Universal Design for Learning (UDL) Guidelines. But since she didn't really understand what they were and no one was emphasizing them, she'd glossed over that Guideline.

This window into the significance of executive functioning reset Lisa's entire career. A few months later, she began a fellowship at Kennedy Krieger Institute to learn more about the developing brain and the neuroscience of learning and behavior, which enabled her to deepen her research and understanding of executive functioning and how it relates to education. After her fellowship ended, Lisa stayed on at the institute and served as an education consultant working to bridge the divide between what medically focused researchers and practitioners knew about the developing brain and what teachers were taught. As part of her work, Lisa conducted a study that showed that only 24% of teachers reported learning about executive functions within their coursework, which explains why the concept feels a bit fuzzy for so many of us (Carey et al., 2020). Soon she became determined to address this worrisome gap in teacher education; specifically, she began to put together professional development sessions, blog posts, conference presentations, massive open online courses, and even a dissertation—all on executive functioning.

As she delved further into the importance of executive functions, she started to offer fellow UDL practitioners and educators a more nuanced understanding of executive functions and how to build learning environments that support the development of and competency in this critical set of skills. At one particular UDL conference, she met Alexis Reid, an educator and learning specialist focused on helping students, teachers, and families understand and further develop executive functioning skills. Alexis and Lisa quickly recognized that they were both motivated to expand educator awareness and understanding of executive functions, and this was the beginning of a long-lasting partnership (and friendship!).

Alexis had encountered the same gap in her teacher training when it came to learning about executive functions. Though her undergraduate work at Loyola University in Baltimore focused on the *cura personalis*, or "care for the whole person," the term *executive functioning* was not explicitly addressed. Later, Alexis expanded her studies of developmental and educational psychology, adding a focus on the developing brain to better understand the underlying neurological and psychological mechanisms that both support and impact the development of executive functions. Ultimately, during her graduate studies at Boston College, Alexis found herself translating the research of neurocognitive, clinical, and developmental psychologists into practice. While interning and later working as a

CAST Cadre and National Faculty member at CAST, Alexis deepened her connection with UDL and began integrating the framework into all that she does. This led to her work directly implementing what she learned in the classroom for many years in Boston, and later alongside incredible therapists who are committed to helping children, adolescents, young adults, and adults get back on track with learning and life. As an educational therapist, learning consultant, and adjunct professor, Alexis is dedicated to bridging the gap between learning and wellness to share what she has studied theoretically, as well as what she has experienced through research and practice, with caregivers, educators, and learners of all ages to help them better understand and support executive functions. When educators, caregivers, and learners alike learn more about executive functioning and what helps, it transforms not only their educational experiences but also many other aspects of their lives.

★ ★ ★

With a shared passion for expanding educators' awareness and understanding of executive functioning, we now spend our careers advocating for the support of executive functions across educational contexts and the life span. Through proactive and interventional aid, psychoeducation, professional development, conference presentations, and authorship of articles, chapters, and now this book, we are committed to promoting the impressive and important set of cognitive skills that support anyone taking on complex tasks in learning and life.

Indeed, this book is the outgrowth of our work developing more effective ways to translate the relevance of executive functioning for fellow educators and address this gap in teacher training. We believe that when teachers understand how these skills develop and show up in learning environments, they are better prepared to address obstacles their learners encounter *and* better able to teach these skills to their learners.

Further, we are motivated by our joint passion to help all learners succeed through better understanding of how their own executive functioning skills play an important role in their academic, social, and health outcomes. Looking back, it's no accident that we met while attending a UDL conference, where we realized we were "speaking the same language" not just about UDL, but about executive functioning. We saw immediately how UDL provided a clear way to build executive functioning skills inside and outside the classroom. The UDL framework not only guides educators to proactively plan for learning variability—and therefore increase the opportunities for meaningful, equitable learning experiences—but also helps educators and learners recognize executive functioning as a key factor in successful learning.

We also believe it is imperative that educators appreciate the fact that this set of cognitive and emotional skills can be supported and developed over time. Think about the way in which you navigate your day: Are there tools, systems, or approaches that help you juggle the multiple facets of your life? To be an educator means that we are constantly organizing, planning, monitoring, and reflecting to establish meaningful learning environments, connections, and opportunities for creativity. Over time, and with experience, we begin to figure out what's helpful (and what's not) to accomplish tasks, work toward goals, and ultimately find an appropriate balance to achieve a positive sense of well-being within and beyond learning environments. When we know what to do, we feel good and can tackle even the most challenging situations.

Over the years, we have amassed an incredible collection of empirically based strategies and approaches to guide and support learners' executive functions. But we know from experience that simply listing off strategies is far less useful than empowering educators with deeper knowledge of executive functions, how they develop, and what types of environmental factors support or detract from learners being able to use these critical skills to their maximum capacity. No two learning contexts are the same. No two learners are the same. For this reason, a list of strategies that prescribes what to do will never support the needs of all educators or their learners. But if we understand executive functions on a deeper level, if we can think critically about what aspects of them require support for students who struggle, and if we develop the ability to talk with learners about their own executive functioning, we can reach a greater number of learners in a more meaningful way than any list of strategies ever could.

UDL asks us to consider the essential variability of learners and contexts and to develop a more flexible understanding of the role of learning environments. It also asks us to be conscious of and intentional about how factors that influence a student's executive functioning skills do not operate in isolation. The extent to which skills are utilized is influenced by the context of the learning environment, which includes task demands, embedded supports, materials, and aspects of the physical space (Fischer et al., 1993). As UDL suggests, we must focus on designing learning environments that are ready and responsive to meet the needs of learners, rather than expecting learners to be ready to meet the demands of their learning environment.

How This Book Works

When planning this book, we focused first on establishing foundational knowledge for K–12 educators about executive functions, how they develop from early childhood to young adulthood, and how best to design supportive learning environments that are responsive to the development of these critical skills. "Provide options for Executive Functions" is included as a Guideline within the UDL framework with good reason. It is our goal for this book to empower UDL implementation through a deeper understanding of executive functioning skills and knowledge of what types of options for support are most meaningful at different stages of a student's K–12 journey. The chapters in Part I, "Understanding Executive Functioning," are designed to help you better understand executive functions, identify signs that students are struggling with executive functions and in need of additional support, and recognize how executive functions develop during the K–12 years. In Part II, we share examples of practical ways to develop and support students' executive functioning. This section will provide tips, suggestions, and steps for putting into action what you've learned in Part I.

We acknowledge that with each new adjustment made in education, you might feel like you don't have the time, resources, or room in the curriculum to add or do anything more. While you're engaging in the work to support executive functioning development in your learning environment, we encourage you to consider how to make smaller adjustments to what you already do in order to reduce the additional time and resources needed later. Often, smaller short-term adjustments can lead to long-term improvements. With appropriate supports integrated into the classroom environment and culture, students will feel more comfortable taking the time they need to pause and organize themselves. Having the time and space to manage the information they are receiving and processing internally through their minds and bodies, as well as externally from their environment, enables them to create more efficient plans, monitor their own progress, and think flexibly as they take on increasingly complex tasks or creative risks over time. Rather than doing the work for our learners or overdoing the options that we provide, we want to simplify systems in order to establish the accessible conditions that support their executive functioning development and independence to navigate each day. These strategies are intended to target some of the behaviors that learners, regardless of age or circumstance, may struggle with as they are developing, strengthening, or aiming to fully activate their executive functions.

We hope that Part II helps you to rectify some of the questions or concerns that you have about how to best support executive functioning skills in the learning environment you work within. For more information or to participate in the conversation, you can visit us at *https://reidconnect.com/* or email us at *Alexis@ReidConnect.com* and *Carey@KennedyKrieger.org*.

PART I
Understanding Executive Functioning

1
SIGNS OF STRUGGLE

Without signs of struggle, executive functions can easily remain invisible, working behind the scenes in our students' minds. Indeed, nothing makes executive functions easier to observe and consider than when things just aren't running smoothly. In a 2019 study, Dr. Lisa Keenan and her colleagues asked Irish primary school teachers about their knowledge of executive functions and provided training on the subject. After learning that executive functions are a set of cognitive control skills (inhibitory control, working memory, and cognitive flexibility) used when tasks are unfamiliar or unpracticed, the teachers shared that it was easiest to understand the concept of executive functions by first considering examples of students struggling with these cognitive skills (Keenan et al., 2019). So here we are.

Although you might not have formal training in executive functions, research has emphasized that most teachers have worked with learners who struggled to use their executive functioning skills effectively. Like most teachers, Lisa had experiences with students struggling with executive functions before she ever heard the term.

Lisa met "Greg" early in her career as a special education teacher in Baltimore County Public Schools. Greg was a bright, engaged, articulate 11th-grade student with an individualized educational plan (IEP) for dyslexia, for which he received accommodations and interventions. After a month of school, it became clear that reading and writing were not the primary reasons for his academic struggles. Greg would attend class ready to discuss the assigned reading and make connections between the text and current events or past readings. He encouraged discussion and debate within the class. Greg was clearly absorbing the material, making meaning, and applying his knowledge with great skill. His independent work completion, however, was nonexistent.

In each class, this bright, engaged student had zeros splattered all over his grade report. Lisa sat down with Greg and discussed what was going on. He described having difficulty completing tasks and often forgetting to turn in work he *had* completed. He also described feeling distracted and having trouble dealing with his frustrations with writing. At the time, having no training or familiarity with executive functioning, Lisa labeled Greg as having "issues with organization." To help him, she created organization and reminder systems. She also discussed strategies and alternative ways to deal with his frustration or remember to follow through with tasks. Lisa suggested that when he began to feel frustrated, he should try taking a break to walk and breathe before returning to a difficult task.

Years later, as Lisa sat in a seminar about executive functioning, her mind went straight to Greg and his struggles. His difficulty hadn't been knowledge acquisition; it was that he needed help managing assignments and getting tasks done. At the time, Lisa didn't understand that Greg was experiencing what our colleagues in psychology and neuroscience refer to as *executive dysfunction*. She hadn't realized that he struggled to use inhibitory control to pause and shift his responses when he became frustrated. She didn't recognize his disorganization as a need for more working memory supports. Lisa had guessed at some solutions to support him (and admittedly, she'd been a bit lucky). The fact that Greg was a thoughtful, self-aware teenager had made her task much easier. Receiving nuanced information about executive functioning enabled Lisa to better identify and create targeted supports to assist other learners who didn't yet possess the same introspective skills as Greg.

What Is Executive *Dys*function?

All skills—riding a bike, driving, tying a shoe, as well as cognitive skills—are dynamic and responsive to the environment in which we attempt to use them. A competent swimmer may struggle to swim in rough, open waters if all they've ever done is practice in a pool. A highly skilled educator may struggle to guide students when simultaneously managing a family crisis. How well our students are able to utilize their skills to facilitate learning is heavily dependent upon the situation (Fischer & Rose, 1994). For example, a young student may be able to attend to a lesson and sit still on a rug for 10 minutes of instruction but will struggle to do the same when the lesson is expanded to 45 minutes. These examples illustrate that the ways in which we demonstrate our skills are highly dependent upon the context. When we describe learners struggling with executive functions, we *must* keep the dynamic nature of skills in mind.

The term *executive dysfunction* is *not* a diagnosis or static label. As with any skill, some of us of have very strong executive functioning skills and some of us have weaker skills, but executive dysfunction is about the relationship between the person and their environment, not the person alone. The term is used to describe moments and contexts in which a person is struggling to match their executive functioning skills to the situation. This mismatch of skill to demand can happen to *anyone*.

We recognize that this term carries with it a heavy clinical tone. We had lengthy discussions about using the term in this book and ultimately decided to include it because it's used in the peer-reviewed literature about executive functioning. We wanted to empower you with terminology that would allow you to engage in further reading on the topic and to communicate effectively with related service providers, such as school psychologists, as well as learners' medical providers (when necessary). UDL encourages us to consider the ways in which the learning environment must change to remove barriers so that all students can thrive. With that in mind, we encourage you to think of symptoms of executive dysfunction as signs of potential trouble in your learning environments and the unmet needs of your students.

To start, let's think diagnostically about our learning environments. What are the symptoms telling us? How do we best create a course of treatment for learning spaces, materials, and lessons? Signs of executive dysfunction are often referred to as "behavioral indicators," which can be any number of ways that a student is struggling to use their executive functioning skills in a certain context. Learning to spot behavioral indicators of executive dysfunction enables us to intervene and make changes to the learning environment. It's important to note that we include instruction within our conceptualization of the learning environment. It's not enough to offer supports for executive functions; we must teach our learners the skills and strategies to support their own executive functioning as they move toward skillful independence.

What Are the Behavioral Indicators of Executive Dysfunction?

Some of the established behavioral indicators associated with executive dysfunction are impulsivity, distractibility, difficulty completing complex tasks, difficulty transitioning between activities, and difficulty shifting patterns of thought (Gioia et al., 2015). Let's unpack each of these behaviors a bit.

Impulsivity

In the in-person learning environment, "calling out" rather than following classroom procedures for sharing speaking time (such as raising a hand, or in a classroom with students who are Blind, calmly stating your name before sharing your response) is probably the most frequently mentioned example of impulsivity. Impulsivity is a sign that a student is struggling to use their inhibitory control—the executive functioning skill that allows us to pause or stop when our initial reaction isn't the best idea for the situation. As we'll see in later chapters, inhibitory control is the first of the executive functions to develop and works as a foundation for the others. Pausing long enough to adjust behavior is the foundation of using the other executive functions. We often hear educators describe "problem behaviors" that they view as intentional on the learners' part, but upon closer inspection, these behaviors (calling out, slamming objects in frustration, shouting at a peer, not stopping when told to do so, becoming irritable when changes to a plan occur) are often related to struggles with inhibitory control.

Distractibility

Distractibility can be tricky to notice. Some learners are engaged in off-task behaviors that are quite obvious to a teacher, such as moving around the room, fiddling with objects, or chatting with peers. Others, however, are distracted in a daydreamy sense, which is less obvious. Even more complicated is trying to identify distracted learners in a virtual setting! Distracted students often struggle with following directions because they didn't attend to them in the first place. This can also be related to distractions caused by sensory stimuli in the environment (sights, sounds, smells, sensations, etc.) or internal dysregulation (emotionally or physiologically) as well as disorganized thinking. Struggling to socialize due to missed verbal and body-language cues from others can be another sign of distractibility.

Difficulty Completing Complex Tasks

The complexity of a task is relative to the learner's age, intellectual ability, background knowledge, and amount of practice or familiarity with the task. For example, a high school student who has been tying their shoe independently for a decade is unlikely to use executive functioning skills to do so. For them, the task is so automatic that they don't need to use cognitive control skills to work through the process. For someone first learning to tie their shoe, however, this task requires keeping multiple steps in mind while executing fine motor skills, using inhibitory control to pause and regulate emotional responses, and thinking flexibly when a first attempt is unsuccessful. There are many reasons why a learner may not complete a complex task.

In order to determine if a learner is struggling to complete tasks due to executive dysfunction, we must first determine if they have the knowledge necessary to complete the task. For example, if a child is struggling to tie their shoe, it's important to first see if they have the procedural knowledge or previous experiences to do so. Next, we should consider if the task requires executive functioning skills (i.e., an unpracticed skill that requires inhibitory control, working memory, or cognitive flexibility). Finally, it is important to determine where the learner got "stuck." If a learner had the necessary tools and academic or technical skills to complete the task, it is important to consider how adjusting executive functioning demands and supports might help them with task completion.

Difficulty Transitioning Between Activities

When educators speak of difficulty with transitions, we often approach the issue as related to will, rather than skill. For example, a teacher may say, "He doesn't like to transition from math to reading," or, "She's upset by transitioning to lunch." These labels not only are misleading but often ignore the nature of the transition, as there may be more complex processes involved than students have previously experienced—in other words, they require cognitive flexibility. It's therefore important to consider that shifting from tasks and contexts requires inhibitory control (stopping the original task), working memory (keeping the final steps or rules of the first task in mind while simultaneously planning for the next task), and cognitive flexibility (considering how behaviors will need to change and how to interact in a new context).

Difficulty Shifting Patterns of Thought

One of the best examples of difficulty with shifting patterns of thought is a learner who is completing a set of multiplication problems, then comes across a division problem and continues to multiply. In this instance, the conceptualization of dealing with the numbers through multiplication has become almost automatic. While we sometimes think of continuing to multiply as a "careless error," it's also the case that the learner had to pause and shift their thinking. Cognitive flexibility skills are also required when students are asked to consider someone else's point of view; shifting from their own perspective to someone else's can cause difficulty for a student struggling with executive functioning. Another example of a learner showing difficulty in shifting patterns of thought is when they're asked to perform a mental manipulation, such as considering various shapes that make up a pyramid (square base, triangle sides).

Look at the Learning Environment First

As we've mentioned, the learning environment plays a major role in how well learners are able to develop and practice their executive functioning skills. Here are some examples of questions you can ask when evaluating the executive functioning supports in a learning environment:

Are the learners at ease?

Stress negatively impacts executive functioning, while, according to executive functions and development expert Dr. Adele Diamond, joy is a great support for it.

Are instructions clear and delivered in multiple modalities for learners to access after the initial delivery?

Often learners can miss parts of an instruction or direction, causing uncertainty and frustration that can impact executive functioning.

Are timing demands developmentally appropriate and flexible?

Young children shouldn't sit still for direct instruction for longer than 10-minute chunks, and older children often still need frequent movement breaks while working.

Are supporting materials easy to find?

Needs for working memory and cognitive flexibility are variable, and supports should be available to everyone.

Are procedures for transitions specific and practiced?

Reduce working memory load when possible!

Teach Learners to Recognize Executive Dysfunction

Think back to Greg, the introspective student who was able to clearly describe his difficulty keeping on task and finishing assignments due to underlying challenges with executive functioning. Students like Greg can easily compensate for lacking executive functioning skills if they have other strengths, charisma, or skills that they lean on to mask their inability to work efficiently. He could have easily flown under the radar, but luckily, his difficulty was identified and an intervention provided the help he needed. However, because Greg learned and was both able to identify when he became frustrated and open to making some adjustments, he could use strategies that mitigated his executive functioning challenges. For Lisa, this was a powerful lesson. As informed educators, we have the opportunity to destigmatize issues with executive functions and help our students learn to identify and describe when they feel stuck; and when students learn how to manage their executive functioning struggles regularly, they become strong self-advocates and more confident learners. While Greg was a high school student, even very young children and students with developmental disabilities can communicate when they are struggling with executive functions if we teach them how to spot the signs and communicate effectively.

⌔ Notes From the Field

As part of a professional learning project, teachers Tracy Pendred, Megan Dash, and Kimberly Spears of City Neighbors Charter School in Baltimore taught their fourth- and fifth-grade students about executive functioning, including the signs of getting stuck. As a result of this project, students made better use of the executive functioning supports offered within the classroom and engaged in open and caring conversations about diverse learning needs and the moment-to-moment shifts in the learning process. Rather than labeling themselves or others, the students started to see that executive functioning changes all the time based on task, environmental demands, and intrapersonal and interpersonal experiences—and, as a result, their needs for support also vary. The students learned valuable lessons about the other skills that go into the learning process and how to self-advocate for needed supports. They also demonstrated improvements in empathy for their peers. For example, when a student got frustrated, confused about next steps, or stuck on a problem, the other students would gently ask if they wanted to visit the executive functioning resource station.

Why Focus on the Signs of Struggle?

This is a book about supporting student executive functions, so why spend a whole chapter talking about the behaviors associated with executive dysfunction? As we mentioned, the construct of executive functioning is never so clear to us as it is when things are not going well. When learners are successfully utilizing their executive functioning skills, everything runs smoothly and we don't see the mechanisms of their cognitive control skills working behind the scenes. When we think about the signs of struggling with executive functioning, however, we're able to see the gaps in learner skills that need supporting.

In addition to helping us better understand executive functions, discussing the signs of executive dysfunction aids us in evaluating our learning environments and considering when, how, and for whom to add executive functioning supports moment to moment. As our notes from the field demonstrate, teaching learners about executive functioning helps them develop these critical skills while also contributing to fruitful discussions about self-advocacy, flexible learning environments, and the fluidity of skill and ability.

KEY TAKEAWAYS FROM CHAPTER 1

	CHAPTER SUMMARY	**YOUR NOTES**
Why should K–12 educators care about student executive functions?	Executive functions are the bridge between knowing and showing what you know. Our learning environments can create barriers to student executive functions or support and enhance these critical skills.	
What is executive dysfunction?	Executive dysfunction is when an individual's executive functions are mismatched with, and thus unable to meet, the demands of a task. Executive dysfunction is *not* a static condition, nor is it a diagnosis.	
How?	We can support student executive functions by viewing the behavioral indicators of executive dysfunction as symptoms that our learning environments are a mismatch for our students' executive function development and need to be enhanced with more and better executive functioning supports.	

2

WHAT ARE EXECUTIVE FUNCTIONS?

Now that we've thought about signs that students are struggling with executive functions, let's dig in and build a more nuanced understanding of the concept. Executive functions are often defined as a cluster of cognitive skills used to achieve goals—not necessarily big life goals (like becoming a famous musician), but everyday goals, like getting to school on time, completing an assignment, or even opening a locker.

Imagine you're a teacher driving to work. It's 6 a.m. and still dark outside. As you steer your car over familiar roads, you're listening to the radio and thinking through the lessons you'll teach today. Suddenly, you encounter flashing lights and a roadblock. There's been an accident. You're directed to a detour, which takes you to an unfamiliar road.

Now your routine commute feels different, and you need to focus and pay close attention to where you're going. You switch off the radio. You're no longer thinking about today's lessons. All your attention is focused on trying to navigate to the school and get there on time. You feel yourself getting anxious, your heart beating a bit faster. As you drive carefully through the narrow, unfamiliar streets, you take a few long breaths to calm down. When you finally reach your destination, you feel a bit worn out. Today's commute took far more effort than usual.

Anyone who travels to work knows the difference between the automatic routines of a daily commute and the added cognitive demands required when an unexpected event suddenly grabs your attention and triggers a reaction. An accident, a blocked road, a delayed train—such interruptions can easily force us out of the realm of automatic routines and calm thinking and into a headspace that feels a bit more stressful and requires more effortful thinking in order to accomplish the end goal—in this case, getting to work on time.

The difference between a routine morning in which you can glide by on autopilot and the more effortful thinking required by an unrehearsed situation illustrates the brain's use of executive functions. When things were going smoothly during your imagined drive to work, you were able to spend cognitive effort on thinking about the day ahead. As soon as detours were thrown into the mix, taking you down literal unknown paths, your cognitive effort was redirected. You had to stop driving on autopilot and instead think and act purposefully, holding information about the situation in mind while following detour signs, navigating the unfamiliar roads, and considering possible alternative routes. You also needed to notice the rising tide of anxiety, which would only have made it harder to think and react to this new situation, and pause to engage a deep breathing strategy. Collectively, these various steps of dealing with a novel situation are executive functions.

Just as in the commute example, we all use our executive functions on a daily basis to accomplish tasks that require a bit more purposeful effort. For example, a sixth grader trying to open their locker will recruit their executive functions to hold the combination in mind while thinking about turning the dial clockwise first, to pause and remember to turn the dial counterclockwise next, and to pause again to remember to turn the dial clockwise for the final number. They'll also have to use their executive functions to remember to recruit calming strategies as they get frustrated and to think flexibly about solutions if the locker still won't open. (By the way, we can make this and other tasks easier and less stressful for our students, and we intend to use this book to explain why and how.)

We rely on our executive functions throughout our lives and across multiple contexts—for everything from grocery shopping to logging in to a medical records portal. We use these cognitive control skills to get tasks done, especially when they are new to us. While we need our executive functions in many situations, they are absolutely critical within learning environments. In fact, students' executive functioning is more predictive of later academic outcomes than any measure of IQ (Fitzpatrick, 2014).

As teachers, we purposefully push students out of the realm of the automatic, constantly introducing new information, teaching new skills, and demanding higher levels of mastery. Indeed, this is what we *should* be doing; it's the very nature of teaching and learning to ask our students to adjust to new information, absorb its significance, and apply it. However, this dynamic—of us always moving the bar a bit out of reach and students always needing to adjust—forever places our students in the position of the disrupted daily commute. By forcing learners out of the automatic and routine, we require them to use their executive functions to higher degrees in the classroom than they might need to in their personal lives. For this reason, it is important that we understand executive functions, how they develop, how we can better support them, and how we can teach students about this valuable set of skills.

The Core Executive Functions

Countless researchers and clinicians have worked to both define and identify executive functions. As mentioned earlier, there are a few different ways of conceptualizing executive functions, but it's generally agreed that they comprise skills that assist with behaviors used for purposefully accomplishing a task. The research literature refers to executive functions as "a set of cognitive control skills" (Nigg, 2017; Perone et al., 2021), which is a technical way of saying thinking skills we use with effort (and on purpose) to control our behaviors and emotions and get stuff done.

Given the latest research (our own as well as that of others), and through our teaching and clinical experience, we believe that developmental neuropsychology offers educators the most comprehensive and constructive way to approach executive functions for the purposes of teaching students in the K–12 setting. Neuropsychologists, the members of the neuroscience field that link brain and behavior to help us understand the biological bases of how we think, learn, and act, have been researching the set of skills referred to as executive functions for decades (Nigg, 2017). In this book, we will focus on the core executive functions of *inhibitory control, working memory,* and *flexible thinking* (Diamond, 2013), while also keeping in mind that no skill functions in isolation from its context or the rest of the body-mind systems, such as other cognitive skills, emotions, or even the gut (Doebel, 2020). This means that while we'll focus on the core executive functions, we'll do so in a way that acknowledges their interactive nature with one another, the rest of the human body and mind, and the context in which our students live and learn. We also take a developmental approach to executive functions and always keep in mind that since they develop over the course of a student's life, it's important to match demands and supports for executive functioning to students' developmental readiness.

Inhibitory Control

Inhibitory control is the ability to intentionally prevent a behavior before it starts, or pause or stop it soon after it starts, so that it doesn't interfere with a purposeful activity or goal. Keeping in mind that executive functions are the set of skills necessary for completing goal-directed tasks, we can think of inhibitory control as the mechanism that allows us to stop any behaviors that might get in the way of completing those tasks (Diamond, 2013). Let's think about a real classroom example. Imagine a student trying to pay attention to a demonstration about mixing chemicals in their science class. Their phone buzzes in their pocket, but they stop themselves before picking it up to look at it.

We can visualize inhibitory control as a stoplight. Imagine a child trying to cross a busy street. The cars on the road are interfering with their ability to safely cross. A stoplight comes on to prevent the interference of the cars and provide a pathway for the child. Inhibitory control functions like a stoplight, stopping interference as learners engage with a task.

Common ways that a student might demonstrate a lack of inhibitory control include:

- Blurting out an answer while a teacher questions another student

- Slamming a laptop shut out of frustration

- Shoving another student who accidentally stepped on their foot in the hallway

All of these examples can be due to inhibitory control failing to allow the student to pause and choose a more appropriate response.

Want to see inhibitory control in action? Play "go/no-go games" with students (or adults!). These are games that require participants to stop a behavior that would have otherwise been automatic. Simon

Says is a great example of a go/no-go game that requires participants to use their inhibitory control skills (and is a proven way to develop inhibitory control; see Chapter 3 for more details). In this game, the automatic response would be to do whatever the leader says to do. But to win, players must only do what the leader says when they start their command with the phrase "Simon says." That means there are times in the game when players should *not* follow the leader's directions. Thus, to win, players must pause and inhibit their response to the leader's command.

Inhibitory control sets the stage for the other executive functioning skills. It is the first of these skills to develop, but it must continue to develop as situations and context demands become more complex. Successful use of inhibitory control will look different throughout the life span. A kindergarten student might use lots of inhibitory control to stay in their assigned spot on the rug for 10 minutes of direct instruction, while a high school student may perform the same task with minimal effort. Remember that executive functioning skills are always context dependent and can vary from person to person and moment to moment depending on what's happening both internally and externally.

Working Memory

Working memory is the cognitive ability to hold multiple pieces of information in mind while purposefully manipulating that information (Nigg, 2017). For example, a student needs to use working memory to remember directions while starting a task. Working memory plays a large role in performing academic tasks.

For early and emerging readers, working memory plays a large role in decoding unfamiliar words. Students must keep each letter's sound in mind as they approach the next and then put all the sounds together to form the word. If they're trying to read a sentence, they must keep each word in mind as they decode the next and then put all the information together to form the sentence. Because our executive functions are used when tasks aren't automatic, practice and memorization of letter sounds and sight words decrease the demands on working memory over time. By the time most students become proficient readers, the types of text they are asked to read become more complex, creating a more demanding situation that once again requires working memory skills (Denckla, 2018).

Common areas where weaknesses in working memory might show up in the classroom include:

- Holding pieces of a story in mind to answer questions about plot and characterization

- Holding directions and passwords in mind while trying to log in to a new LMS (learning management system)

- Recalling all of the physical positioning directions while staying attuned to where in the piece the rest of the music class is singing to prepare for a solo

- Remembering their assigned homework while standing at their locker and thinking through what materials to take home for the weekend

Working memory is also critical for completing math problems and constructing written responses, which means that it's crucial for enabling a learner's ability to successfully demonstrate mastery. Working memory capacity varies not only with development but also within certain contexts, and it can impact student academic success even when the learner knows the required information. For instance, even though a student has prepared for a test and knows the information well, if they become particularly anxious beforehand, their working memory capacity may be hampered and they may not perform as well as they should. This can also show up as a student missing parts of instruction, directions, or even social cues during conversations. As students get older, they will frequently be asked to follow along by taking notes or jotting down ideas while listening or watching the lesson. This requires a great amount of focus and cognitive control related to holding information in mind to use it in some way. When working memory is compromised or limited, it can impact other factors related to learning and performance. The good news is that researchers have created many strategies to support and improve working memory capacity.

Cognitive Flexibility

Cognitive flexibility, or flexible thinking, is the ability to purposefully adjust thinking to meet the demands of a new context, maintain focus, and complete a goal-directed behavior (Nigg, 2017). Think of cognitive flexibility as the ability to pivot or shift. (In fact, some of the executive functioning literature refers to this skill as *shifting*.) Cognitive flexibility is used to identify the problem that needs solving, consider possible solutions, pick a strategy, monitor the use of the strategy, and then change course if the selected strategy isn't working (Diamond, 2013). Cognitive flexibility is when we start to see how executive functions support strategic thinking!

We might be tempted to think this executive functioning skill is the domain of older learners. But consider how young children experiment with activities like building block towers. The child's goal is to build the highest tower possible, but the tower keeps collapsing! As they play, the child evaluates the problem and tries out different solutions. Maybe a wider base? Maybe bigger blocks on the bottom instead of the top? Eventually, the child figures out a solution to their problem. In addition to feeling proud and having fun, they have also practiced their executive functioning skills!

This example also highlights how the other elements of executive functioning—inhibitory control and working memory—contribute to goal-directed behavior. In order to solve the problem of the tower collapsing, the child must hold in mind what strategies they've tried, what other options might work, and what they see other people do with block towers. Simultaneously, they must inhibit the impulse to throw the blocks in frustration and stop behaviors that might cause the tower to fall down, such as moving their body too much.

> ### ⏱ Notes From the Field
>
> My sister is a huge LEGO fan. When we were kids, I'd shift between awe and jealousy as she quickly glanced at the assembly directions, built the LEGO structure, and then disassembled it to create something even more imaginative and fun to play with. She could hold the plans and shapes in her mind with ease and then think flexibly about how various elements of the original design could be reconfigured. She'd spend hours playing with LEGO bricks (and any other building toy) designing and redesigning—her creations the physical manifestation of flexible thinking.
>
> —Lisa

Older learners also use flexible thinking aided by inhibitory control to complete academic tasks and navigate social situations. (Think of all of the extra problem-solving required to collaborate on a group assignment!) It's important to remember that "problem-solving" isn't just about math problems, but about navigating the many different barriers to meeting our constantly shifting goals throughout the day. From opening tricky lockers to dealing with group work, learners use flexible thinking skills in different learning environments, not just when presented with a specific academic problem to solve.

Other common areas where deficits in cognitive flexibility might show up in the classroom include:

- Staying on-task while being flooded with social media messages and considering an appropriate response to a new social "crisis"

- Remembering the facts prepared for a class debate while considering the arguments of the other team and composing a retort

- Completing a math assignment where the operations (+/−) have changed: pausing, noticing the change, and shifting the approach to the problem

KEY TAKEAWAYS FROM CHAPTER 2

	CHAPTER SUMMARY	YOUR NOTES
Why should educators need to understand executive functions?	As teachers, we purposefully push our students into a state in which tasks are novel or unpracticed (this is how they learn new things), which means students are always using their executive functions!	
What do educators need to know about executive functions?	Executive functions are a set of interactive cognitive control skills used when tasks are unfamiliar or unpracticed. The most commonly agreed-upon core executive functioning skills are inhibitory control, working memory, and cognitive flexibility.	
How will understanding executive functions improve my teaching?	Thinking critically about what executive functions are and the behavioral indicators of executive dysfunction can help us identify when our learning environments are in need of more supports and consider what supports might work best.	

3

EXECUTIVE FUNCTIONS AND THE DEVELOPING BRAIN

Take a moment and place your hand over your forehead. Underneath your hand is the frontal lobe, which contains the prefrontal cortex, a specific area of the brain associated with executive functions. However, no segment of the brain works in isolation, and recent research has emerged showing that other parts of the brain besides the prefrontal cortex also influence executive functions, particularly in children. Specifically, brain imaging studies have demonstrated that the basal ganglia (part of the limbic system) and cerebellum are both very active when children use their executive functions (Loe et al., 2019). UDL illustrates this connection between the frontal lobe (UDL's strategic network) and the limbic system (UDL's affective network) by positioning "self-regulation" and "executive functions" on the same row.

Notice how we said that the prefrontal cortex is *associated* with executive functions. It is important to remember that brains are highly variable. In order to avoid absolutism when discussing brain areas and functions, we use terms like *associated* to remind us that some brains might not fit this model. It also reminds us that the different regions of the brain work together, and that other areas of the brain also influence cognition and behavior.

The human brain is an impressive organ that continues to change throughout the lifetime. While genetics steer brain development, the environment also plays a crucial role. Where a child lives, who they interact with, and the experiences they have all affect the prefrontal cortex and other areas of the brain associated with executive functions. Future chapters will dive into the important role the learning environment plays in helping children and adolescents develop their executive functioning skills, but for now, let's take a quick tour of brain development as it relates to executive functions and learning.

Neurodevelopment and Executive Functions

The prefrontal cortex is the last part of the brain to fully develop, which means that for the entire time students are in K–12 education (as well as undergraduate years for traditional college-age students), the connections within the brain responsible for inhibitory control, working memory, and flexible thinking are still "under construction" (Paus, 2005). One of our favorite analogies about brain development comes from neuropsychologist Dr. Lisa Jacobson: "Neural pathways are like the roads connecting towns within a geographical area. Vehicles can travel unpaved roads and still reach their destination, but not as quickly as they could on well-paved roads. Younger children are working with 'unpaved roads' and hoping to move toward well-constructed highways capable of quick transit of information."

A bunch of students trying to think and learn with "unpaved roads" might sound frustrating to a teacher who is tired of dealing with late and missing assignments, but rather than thinking of a gradually developing prefrontal cortex and neural connections as a barrier to learning, we should consider it a benefit. Because they evolve over time, executive functions are highly influenced by their environment. Therefore, as educators, we have the power to shape and support executive functioning in many ways so that students can achieve academic and social success!

But let's pause for a moment. What do we mean when we talk about brain development? When we say that the prefrontal cortex is still developing beyond the age of 20, what does that say about executive functioning skills inside and outside the classroom? How does this gradual development affect learning?

Averages can be tricky things. For example, averages of cortical growth and development are based on findings from a lot of brain scan data. Each child's scan is added in with the rest of the population and then divided to find these averages. This can be very helpful in some cases, but averages tend to hide variability within the population. There is a wide range of what's "normal" for brain development. So, for example, when we report that on average girls develop faster than boys, that in *no way* means that this is the case every time!

Early Childhood (PreK–Grade 2)

After birth, the brain grows rapidly, with the child's head growing to accommodate the increasing brain size (Kolb & Whishaw, 2021). (Just think about the difference in head size between an infant and a two-year-old!) What's causing this growth is the formation of new brain cells, or neurons. Much of the development happens in the cortex (the outer part of the brain associated with cognition). The brain continues to grow as new neural networks are formed. The process of neurodevelopment does not occur linearly; rather, the human brain grows in much the same way as the rest of the human body—in spurts!

This time of rapid growth, however, doesn't mean that the connections between brain cells are efficient. (We're still dealing with lots of unpaved roads.) So, while young children are gaining skills, they aren't always able to think quickly or make connections between various experiences and pieces of information to form new ideas. For example, a young child might not be able to quickly adjust to different rules in a new setting, like going from home to the library or the playground to the classroom.

As the brain's cortex is growing new neurons, young children start to develop their core executive functions (Diamond, 2013; Korkman et al., 2013). Young children begin learning to use inhibitory control (think of parents teaching toddlers not to hit or bite when frustrated), working memory (like when young kids remember the rules of a simple game while playing), and flexible thinking (which we often see when children are attempting to "troubleshoot" or get around and into things—especially when they shouldn't).

As children age, their core executive functioning skills improve as they accumulate experience, practice, and modeling from adults and older children. In other words, when young children are situated in learning environments that are developmentally appropriate and pose the right amount of challenge, they are given the opportunity to practice and improve their executive functioning skills (part II of this book covers how to create this type of learning environment).

While all of the core executive functioning skills are developing at this time of great neurogenesis, a young child's immature inhibitory control can present a barrier to practicing the other executive functioning skills. For example, if a student isn't able to sit still and attend to the teacher, they'll miss out on what was said, and they won't be able to practice holding that information in their working memory or thinking flexibly about the information. In order to positively influence young children's executive function development, the learning environment must have developmentally appropriate inhibitory control expectations.

How Do We Strengthen Executive Functioning Skills in Young Children?

As educators, we have no influence over genetics, but we can influence the experiences of children within our learning environments. The primary focus for younger children should be to strengthen their inhibitory control. We can help children develop this skill in fun ways (in fact, having fun helps with most learning!). Go/no-go games—such as Simon Says; Red Light, Green Light; and Freeze Dance—have been shown to help students practice inhibiting their first reactions to stimuli. Incorporating these games into the school day can serve the dual purpose of providing much-needed movement breaks as well as enhancing students' inhibitory control skills. Please be mindful that most of these games involve physical responses and actions, so you'll need to adapt them for students for whom physical responses are difficult or not plausible. (We'll dive deeper into ways to support and develop learner executive functioning skills in part II of this book.)

Middle Childhood (Grades 3–6)

The brains of kids in middle childhood are still growing new neurons but not at the same rapid pace as younger children. By age 10 or 11, the average child has almost reached maximum cortical thickness (meaning the outer layer of the brain is as big as it gets). But it's important to remember that brain size does not equal thinking power. Remember those "unpaved roads" of the brain? While kids in middle childhood have grown a lot of new brain cells, there hasn't been much myelination—the development of a fatty sheath that covers brain cells to create more efficient and effective connections, or paved roads. Myelinated brain cells are referred to as *white matter* (because the fatty sheath is white), while unmyelinated brain cells are called *gray matter*. (If it's helpful, you can think white matter = paved and gray matter = unpaved.) So, while kids at this stage have more brain cells than younger children, they tend to have much less white matter than adolescents. What does this mean? Kids in middle childhood have learned a lot and developed a lot of skills, but they don't have very efficient brain networks yet—especially not in the frontal lobe, where most of the executive functioning action takes place!

Middle childhood is often the time in which the differences in executive functions among students become more obvious. As some children become better at avoiding distractions, not blurting out the first thing on their minds, remembering to raise their hands, and waiting for their turn, it can become even more clear which students are still working on these skills. Learners who are still developing these skills can lead some teachers to assume that they're exhibiting signs of an educational disability when they're not. For example, we've had multiple teachers come to us about first graders struggling to attend to whole-class, teacher-led instruction for over 30 minutes, concerned that the children might have an educational disability like ADHD. But when we encourage the teachers to change their expectations to be more in line with students' developmental readiness, the same children are better able to attend, initiate tasks, stay on task, inhibit inappropriate behaviors, and complete their assignments.

It's often been said that every behavior tells some story. Rather than making an assumption about why a learner is struggling or acting a certain way, try to determine if there's something else preventing them from engaging in the work. Be curious about the specific behavior or situation. Ask yourself: Are there skills that haven't been fully developed or solidified? Is there something in the environment that may be triggering this behavior? Might there be an underlying fear, worry, or other variable at play?

Oftentimes, collecting more data before making an assumption can transform an experience and equip you to help the learner realize that in every challenge, they can find support and shift their struggle from an "argh" of frustration to an "a-ha!" of understanding.

Pause a moment and think about the differences in the size of your students. Middle-childhood classrooms often include some kids who look older than their age and some who look younger than first graders. This time of life is quite variable in all aspects of bodily growth—and that includes brain development. (We're not suggesting the size of a child is in any way the same as their brain development, just that various bodily systems develop at different times and at different rates for different people.)

Kids in middle childhood know so much information that it can be tempting for teachers to associate their being knowledgeable with their being able to use executive functioning skills. And because we have higher expectations of students who show good understanding of content, it's easy to misinterpret issues with executive functioning, such as weak inhibitory control, as misbehavior. Misbehavior implies that the student is *choosing* not to raise their hand or to get out of their seat and roam the classroom. When teachers view a lack of inhibitory control as misbehavior, they often seek to control it through punishment. For students who are still developing inhibitory control, punishment is not the best path for helping them develop better skills, and the prospect of punishment can also have a negative impact on their feelings toward school and learning. It's important that teachers and administrators recognize when students are struggling with executive functions and provide supports and instruction to assist them rather than enforce behavioral consequences that might harm a student's natural desire to learn.

Early Adolescence (Grades 7–9)

Early adolescence tends to fall around the time students are in middle school (also known as junior high). If you teach or have taught middle school, then you know that kids of this age seem to be what we lovingly call "uniquely dysregulated." Many people tend to blame puberty: "It's the hormones!" While it's clear that fluctuations in hormones don't help our early adolescents regulate their behavior, there are neurological reasons for our early adolescent students to struggle.

Enter one of our favorite terms in neurodevelopment: *pruning*. To put this concept in the least clinical terms possible, pruning is the stage in brain development in which the brain decides that quality is better than quantity. Underutilized brain cells start to be targeted for *programmed cell death* (another great term) and die off. This leaves room for creating better, faster, stronger brain networks—in other words, pruning helps brains function more efficiently. This process results in brains that are better able to make connections, self-regulate, and optimize executive functions. Students are still learning and developing while their brains are engaged in pruning, but executive functioning development may slow down. As any middle school teacher can tell you, patience is key to supporting the development of early adolescents!

While there are brain-related reasons why students may struggle with executive functions, contextual demands also play a role. Just as the brain is trying to focus on quality rather than quantity, many schools throw a bunch of non-academic learning demands at early adolescent students. Expectations like navigating hallways and lockers independently, changing classes, being assigned more homework, and facing different types of assessments can be difficult for students who are still improving their executive functioning skills. Further, when those demands are perceived as too challenging, it's impossible for students to practice new skills, including those related to executive functions. Rather than slowly building competence and independence, they start to struggle—unnecessarily. Thus, it's important for teachers to keep in mind that this sudden uptick in demands can put stress on still-developing systems and to provide appropriate supports. This isn't just about helping students function in middle school; it's about setting a strong foundation for independent learning in high school and beyond.

Adolescence (Grades 10–12)

If you've taught high school, you've probably observed a wonderful phenomenon at the start of the school year: Many 10th-grade students who couldn't follow multistep directions in ninth grade are suddenly independently making cross-curricular connections and expressing impressively well-thought-out ideas. Why this shift? Myelination.

Adolescence coincides with greater amounts of myelination (Paus, 2005). This means that for high school students, pathways in the brain are becoming faster and more efficient. (We've finally started paving more roads!) But while our high school students are building more efficient brains, they're still not as fast as adult brains. In fact, as one somewhat amusing study from Vanderbilt University points out, when we exclaim, "What were you thinking?" to our high school students, the answer is often that teens are thinking *a lot*, just inefficiently rather than not at all (Baird et al., 2005).

The teenage years are often thought of as a time when adolescents experiment with a greater degree of independence. This is important for brain development, but don't confuse more independence with students being able to function on their own. Students still need guidance and supports as they navigate the demands of longer assignments, more in-depth subjects, and more complex problem-solving and social dynamics inside and outside the classroom.

> ### ⌖ Notes From the Field
>
> While an individual's executive functioning skills will increase as they get older, context demands also increase. At one point in my life I simultaneously taught middle school and undergraduate students. My fellow teachers and I had spent time purposefully building a middle school environment to support student executive functions, but I had just assumed that the young adults would be fine on their own. That semester, the undergraduate students struggled more with executive functions than my 12-year-old learners.
>
> —Lisa

Be on the lookout for phrases such as "not working to his potential," "she's just being lazy," and "he's a mess." These expressions from both teachers and parents can sometimes point to executive functioning challenges rather than a lack of motivation. The more nuanced demands of high school can draw attention to executive functioning challenges that may have flown under the radar earlier in life, sometimes because the student was perceived to be doing "well enough."

For example, it's much more common for students with ADD hyperactive type to be diagnosed in elementary school than it is for students who exhibit the inattentive type of ADD. "Daydreamy" students who were able to cope with the fewer executive functioning demands earlier in their educational careers may start to flounder as those demands increase (for example, greater independence, more extracurricular activities, and more demanding coursework) during their teenage years.

Often students may be doing "well enough" to get by. In fact, many compensate with other strengths like their personality, verbal or visual reasoning skills, or other skills that mask their executive functioning struggles. These invisible struggles are palpable to those who experience them. Here's how one high school student reflected on their journey: "I think that Executive Functioning skills need to be highlighted and prioritized more. As a student I always thought I wasn't smart because I struggled with the work, but when it was broken down into smaller chunks I always did better. For grades 2–4 I went to extra help every week because I never understood what was happening in class, and never once did [it] stand out to my school or teachers that maybe I needed some support. In high school I finally got tested for an IEP (better late than never, I guess!) and it wasn't well done, so I still didn't get the support I needed. Now that I work with Alexis, I see how I need to work with things, so that way I can learn . . . it just needs to be looked at in a different way sometimes!"

Early Adulthood (Post–High School–Mid-20s)

Brain development slows down in early adulthood (Kolb et al., 2016). We can think about this period as the brain putting the finishing touches on its masterpiece. This also tends to be a period in which learners are experiencing far greater degrees of freedom and independence. For many learners, this increase in independence is a great way to sort out and practice refining executive functions. However, for those who have been struggling with executive functions, this time period can be incredibly frustrating.

For those teaching, mentoring, or parenting young adults, it is important to pay attention to difficulties with inhibitory control, working memory, and flexible thinking that might cause issues with school, work, or social success. The shift from the more structured days of high school to a more open and flexible college schedule can be a lot to handle, and this may be when executive functioning challenges emerge and the need for additional support becomes apparent. College students often report that they've never had to manage their own time, learn so much on their own outside of class, or advocate for things they need to be successful inside and outside of class. Assisting young adults with organization, time management, and planning can be helpful. The expectation is that young adults should "have it all together" as they're entering college or the workforce, but anecdotes across professions indicate that this phase of life is difficult to adjust to for many.

As young adults transition out of school and into the workforce, they're expected to have the skills necessary to contribute to society. If the transition into adulthood doesn't go as smoothly as expected (i.e., if they struggle to learn new tasks at work, manage daily life responsibilities, pay bills, or maintain proper hygiene), it could lead to another set of challenges. To compound those challenges, outside influences from social and traditional media and expectations to take a more traditional path to adulthood can skew their perception of reality. Rather than expecting young adults to *just figure it out*, we should encourage and support them in seeking out mental health treatment, learning skills for managing their day-to-day responsibilities, or finding a mentor to guide them at work.

As one college students says, "Be patient and kind. A lot of young adults want to succeed and do their best, but they may not know how or have the tools to do it, so they get discouraged. A professor that is patient and cares could make all of the difference. Also . . . organize the class and the materials and syllabus really well . . . a lot of people cannot handle things that are not organized, especially in an academic setting. Try to be the professor that you would want."

The most important aspect of neurodevelopment to keep in mind as you consider executive functions is that it's highly variable. While averages can be helpful for diagnostics and research, they can be slightly less helpful for designing learning environments and instruction. Regardless of who you teach, you can be sure that some students will need additional assistance with executive functions. Additionally, knowing what disabilities and life events can place learners at greater risk for executive functioning challenges can help you identify those needs.

As the famed child neurologist Dr. Martha Denckla likes to say, "Brains are as variable as the human face." We all tend to have similar features, in similar places, with similar functions, but they can vary tremendously. Pathways to neurodevelopment may be similar, but environment, life events, and genetics all play a role in the timing. As educators we have the ability to shape the environment and contexts in which students learn and thus play a large role in how well—or not—their executive functions develop. Understanding that variability in neurodevelopment is actually the norm will make us more compassionate and proactive educators.

KEY TAKEAWAYS FROM CHAPTER 3

	CHAPTER SUMMARY	YOUR NOTES
Why should teachers care about brain development?	Considering brain development helps us to think developmentally and make sure that our learning environments are developmentally appropriate for our students.	
What is an easy way to think about brain development?	Neural connections are like roads. Newer connections are unpaved—you can still get where you're going, but it's not a quick or easy path! As brains develop, the roads become paved, making them more efficient and effective ways for information to travel.	
How can I use my understanding of brain development to better support student executive functions?	Pausing to reflect on where your students are in their developmental trajectory can help you to plan more effective learning environments and have more patience with your students. It's certainly easier to deal with the antics of middle schoolers when you consider that their brains are engaged in programmed cell death!	

4

EXECUTIVE FUNCTIONING AND UNIVERSAL DESIGN FOR LEARNING

So far, we've introduced the concepts of executive functioning and dysfunction, looked at the important role context plays in executive functioning expression and development, and explored brain development as it relates to executive functioning. While this is all great information, at the end of the day, educators need to know what to *do* with this knowledge—that is, how to link the neuroscience to their instructional practice. This is where it can be helpful to have a translational bridge (Carey et al., 2020) that shows how to apply and utilize the science in the classroom. As we mentioned in our introduction, we've been using Universal Design for Learning, a research-based framework that not only highlights the importance of executive functions but also offers practical strategies and suggestions that can help foster it in learners.

A Quick Overview of the UDL Framework

UDL consists of evidence-based strategies for improving teaching and learning, as shown in Figure 4.1. The framework is transdisciplinary in that it borrows from multiple fields centered on learning, including educational research emphasizing strategies that positively influence academic outcomes; educational psychology research focused on student needs and support strategies; and cognitive neuroscience and neuropsychological research aimed at determining how learning occurs in the brain and how to manipulate conditions to best support it (Meyer et al., 2014).

The UDL framework is divided into three principles based on general conceptions of how the brain processes information: enhancing student engagement, offering options for representation of context, and providing various means of action and expression. It's important to note that brain structures are highly interconnected and that these three principles do not indicate segments of the brain working in isolation.

Within each principle are three Guidelines. Each Guideline was developed based upon a collection of educational, psychological, and neuropsychological research related to providing students with multiple means of engagement, representation of context, and action and expression, respectively.

There are many networks within the brain, but the UDL framework references three that correspond to the three principles and highlight general patterns of neural connectivity that support different aspects of learning. These are the affective, recognition, and strategic networks.

The *affective network* is related to learner engagement, and the three Guidelines within this principle all relate to supporting the emotional needs of the learner. The *recognition network* is related to the various input the brain receives, processes, and stores into new memories. The Guidelines within this principle are focused

The Universal Design for Learning Guidelines

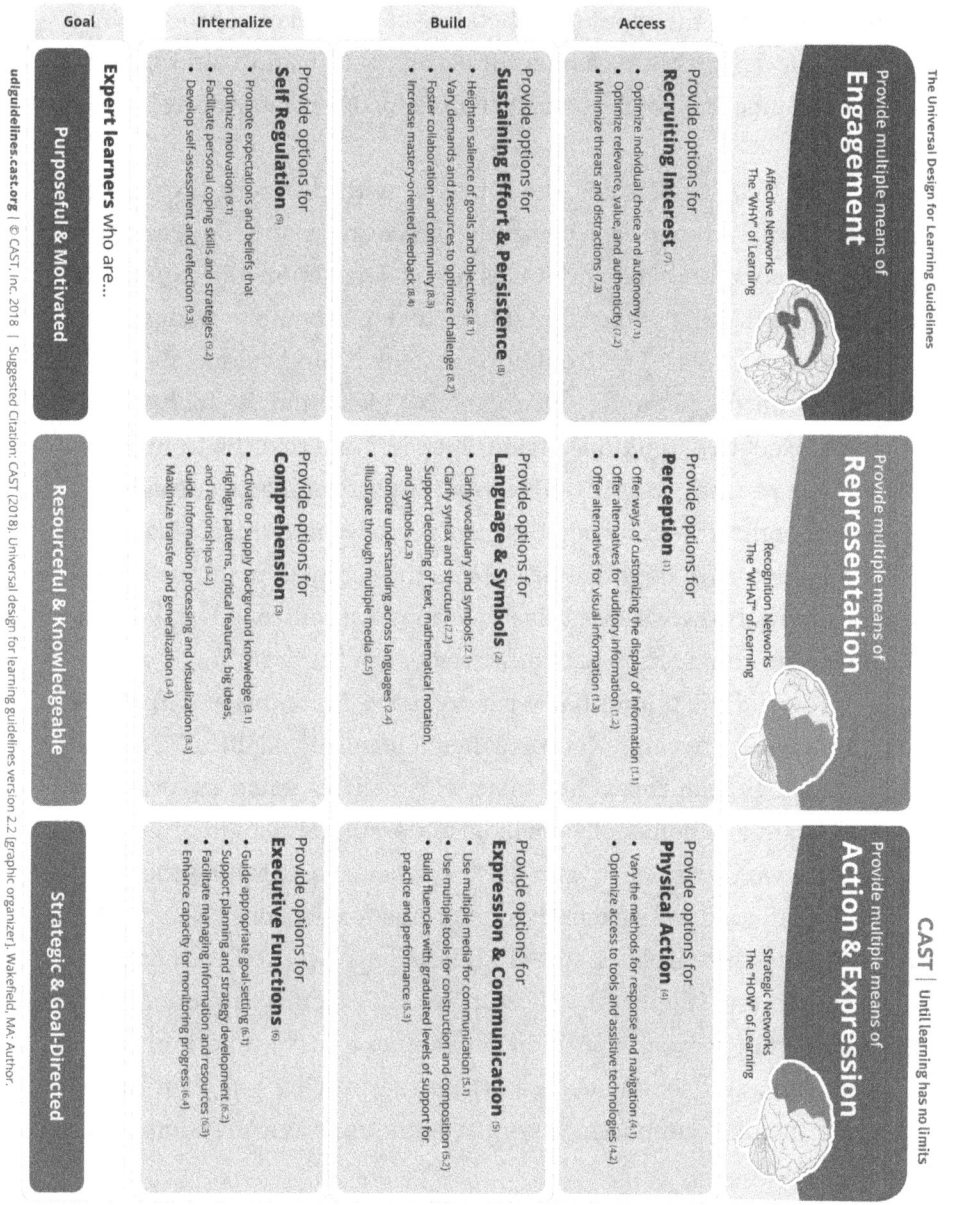

	Access	Build	Internalize	Goal
Provide multiple means of Engagement Affective Networks The "Why" of Learning	**Provide options for Recruiting Interest** (7) • Optimize individual choice and autonomy (7.1) • Optimize relevance, value, and authenticity (7.2) • Minimize threats and distractions (7.3)	**Provide options for Sustaining Effort & Persistence** (8) • Heighten salience of goals and objectives (8.1) • Vary demands and resources to optimize challenge (8.2) • Foster collaboration and community (8.3) • Increase mastery-oriented feedback (8.4)	**Provide options for Self Regulation** (9) • Promote expectations and beliefs that optimize motivation (9.1) • Facilitate personal coping skills and strategies (9.2) • Develop self-assessment and reflection (9.3)	**Expert learners** who are.... **Purposeful & Motivated**
Provide multiple means of Representation Recognition Networks The "WHAT" of Learning	**Provide options for Perception** (1) • Offer ways of customizing the display of information (1.1) • Offer alternatives for auditory information (1.2) • Offer alternatives for visual information (1.3)	**Provide options for Language & Symbols** (2) • Clarify vocabulary and symbols (2.1) • Clarify syntax and structure (2.2) • Support decoding of text, mathematical notation, and symbols (2.3) • Promote understanding across languages (2.4) • Illustrate through multiple media (2.5)	**Provide options for Comprehension** (3) • Activate or supply background knowledge (3.1) • Highlight patterns, critical features, big ideas, and relationships (3.2) • Guide information processing and visualization (3.3) • Maximize transfer and generalization (3.4)	**Resourceful & Knowledgeable**
Provide multiple means of Action & Expression Strategic Networks The "HOW" of Learning	**Provide options for Physical Action** (4) • Vary the methods for response and navigation (4.1) • Optimize access to tools and assistive technologies (4.2)	**Provide options for Expression & Communication** (5) • Use multiple media for communication (5.1) • Use multiple tools for construction and composition (5.2) • Build fluencies with graduated levels of support for practice and performance (5.3)	**Provide options for Executive Functions** (6) • Guide appropriate goal-setting (6.1) • Support planning and strategy development (6.2) • Facilitate managing information and resources (6.3) • Enhance capacity for monitoring progress (6.4)	**Strategic & Goal-Directed**

CAST | Until learning has no limits

udlguidelines.cast.org | © CAST, Inc. 2018 | Suggested Citation: CAST (2018). Universal design for learning guidelines version 2.2 [graphic organizer]. Wakefield, MA: Author.

FIGURE 4.1. The UDL Guidelines (Meyer et al., 2014)

Executive Functioning and Universal Design for Learning   49 on supporting the input and encoding of the learning process. The *strategic network* is necessary for learner action and expression. All of the Guidelines within this principle focus on supporting learner output.

The UDL Guidelines show brains with different highlighted regions at the top of each principle, indicating where the processing for the associated network takes place. The action and expression principle highlights the frontal lobe, which is home to what we call "output controls." The frontal lobe of the brain is associated with motor control, planning and organizing ideas, and the focus of this book: executive functions. Again, keep in mind that the frontal lobe interacts with the rest of the brain while performing these functions. Motor control works when the frontal lobe communicates with the basal ganglia (in the inner brain) and the cerebellum (at the base of the brain). Likewise, executive functions are controlled by the frontal lobe in conjunction with other regions of the brain.

How did the unfamiliar term *executive functions* end up in the framework, anyway? Neuroscience! Or more specifically, neuropsychology. Neuropsychologists, the neuroscience experts that link brain and behavior to help us understand the biological bases of how we think, learn, and act, have been researching the set of skills referred to as executive functions for decades (Nigg, 2017). Countless researchers and clinicians have worked to recognize, measure, and support the development of executive functions. The connection they've identified between executive functioning and academic and social success is one reason why the UDL framework includes supporting executive functions as a key component.

Executive Functions and Self-Regulation

As mentioned earlier, there are many accepted ways of thinking about executive functions, some of which vary among researchers.

While there is agreement that *executive functions* is an umbrella term encompassing various skills that interact and contribute to goal-directed activity, the specific skills in question are sometimes debated (Baggetta & Alexander, 2016; Nigg, 2017). Some models of executive functions include self-regulation skills, while others view self-regulation as a separate set of skills that has a bidirectional relationship with executive functions (Baggetta & Alexander, 2016; Blair, 2016). *Self-regulation* refers to controlling the internal mental and physical states—that is, emotional responses—that help one adapt to various contexts (Nigg, 2017). Models that include self-regulation as part of executive functioning often refer to this as "hot EF," meaning an emotional or affective type of executive functioning (Baggetta & Alexander, 2016).

The UDL framework separates executive functions and self-regulation into two Guidelines. This model of executive functioning aligns with the use of brain region networks to define the UDL principles. Self-regulation is linked to the affective network (i.e., the limbic system), and executive functions are linked to the strategic network (which includes the frontal lobe). While these two Guidelines fall under different principles, they appear on the same row of the framework—an intentional way of showing that they're connected (see Figure 4.2).

In the simplest terms, executive functions and self-regulation affect and support each other. A lack of self-regulation can lead to stress levels that negatively impact the brain's ability to effectively use executive functioning (Diamond, 2013). Likewise, executive functions can enable a learner to remember to use coping skills and strategies when an expression of big emotions might get in the way of completing a task (Blaire & Ursache, 2011).

Remembering the strong link between self-regulation and executive functions will help you understand why many of the UDL recommendations appear to be focused on supporting and developing self-regulation. Think of self-regulation and executive functions as best friends. Each has its own unique strengths, but they complement each other beautifully.

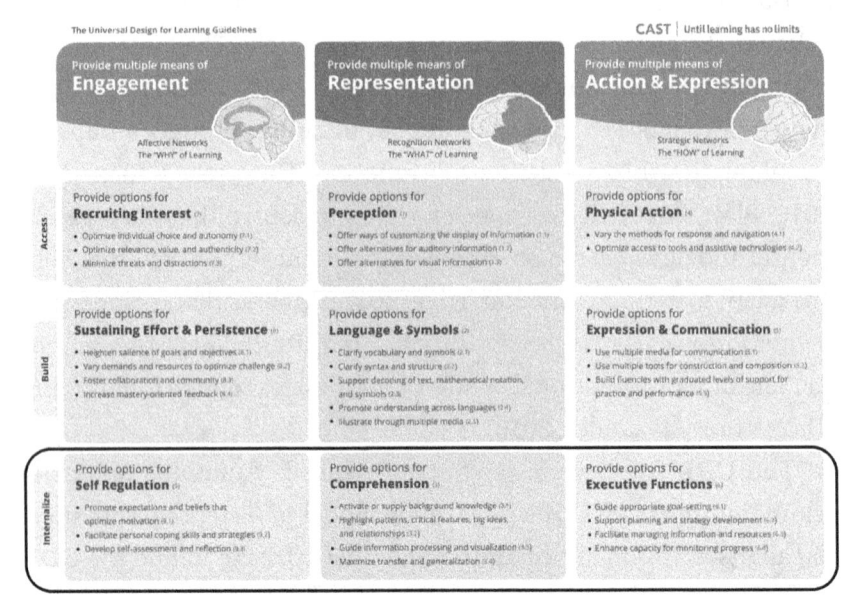

FIGURE 4.2. The connection between the Self-Regulation and Executive Functions Guidelines

Predicting Variability in Executive Functions

UDL asks us to consider neurovariability when we design learning environments. *Neurovariability* refers to how human brains diverge in their makeup and ability. Differences in the human brain are not only normal but also predictable. We know that what is considered typical brain development has a very large range for anticipated executive functioning skill level. Likewise, we know that certain contexts, developmental and learning disabilities, and mental health diagnoses will impact executive functioning. We can use this information to better predict what kinds of executive functioning supports we'll need to plan for within our learning environments.

Self-regulation and executive functions are linked and work together because the affective and strategic networks interact to help maintain a mental and physical state that contributes to completing tasks. When learners struggle to regulate their mood and stress response, it can impact executive functions. It's important to consider that a student's mental health and current mood might mean they need more options for executive functioning supports.

Executive functions are regulated by your brain, and your brain is part of your body, so it follows that executive functions are affected by stressors on your body. Learners experiencing chronic illnesses may struggle with executive functions because of stress, pain, or fatigue. A student with a cold may need some executive functioning supports for the few days they are ill, but one returning from cancer treatment may need these supports for a long time (Carey & Jacobson, 2017).

Understanding a learner means recognizing how a lack of skills or dysregulation of emotions may impact executive functioning activation. It's important to consider all of the potential variables that may be interfering with task initiation, persistence motivation, and task execution.

Learners may have had negative experiences in the past where they didn't yet possess the skills to efficiently navigate a task or challenge. They also may be experiencing anxiety or other mental health challenges that can stifle their process. Those who face frequent barriers from either a skill- or performance-based perspective often describe getting "shut down," "stuck," or "frozen" when trying to do work. This behavior frequently gets labeled as procrastination, laziness, or lack of care. In reality, it may be a lack of skills or a barrier interfering with their performance.

When we face danger, our limbic system alerts our frontal lobes to go into flight, fight, or freeze mode, and the same response can occur when we're faced with a challenge. Anxiety or stress can be triggered by an assignment, assessment, interaction, perception, or situation.

In these moments, it's important to prompt students to reflect on what is needed, take a breath and/or a break, or ask for assistance to regulate their emotions and reactivate executive functioning skills.

It's also important to keep in mind that many treatments for illnesses can impact a student's executive functioning. Some medications, such as anti-epileptic drugs, can cause mental fogginess that diminishes executive functioning. Cancer treatments (in particular when given to pediatric patients) can affect executive functioning and other cognitive developmental skills. (Note: This is *not* to suggest that these treatments shouldn't be given; in most cases they're life-saving medications. We simply want to point out that there are some side effects that educators should be aware of.) Additionally, traumas to the head and brain can impact executive functioning.

Consider the Context

In addition to specific diagnoses related to developmental and learning disabilities, learners can have difficulty with executive functions when context demands are not in sync with their abilities. This can be caused by the environment or by mental and emotional stressors.

UDL asks practitioners to consider the learning environment as the supporter of ability or the cause of disability. Vygotsky (1978) explained this concept with his theory of the Zone of Proximal Development (ZPD). An unsupportive environment will not enable someone to learn, but an environment that is too supportive won't challenge a learner with new skills. The learning environment must strike a balance between support and challenge. The fit of the learning environment in relation to the neurodevelopment of the learner is referred to as *stage-environment fit* (Eccles et al., 1993). We need to consider the environment as a whole and how well the executive functioning demands fit the learner's neurodevelopmental stage and learning tasks, as well as whether they strike a proper balance between support and challenge.

KEY TAKEAWAYS FROM CHAPTER 4

	CHAPTER SUMMARY	YOUR NOTES
Why is it critical that a flexible learning environment offer options for learners' executive functions?	"Provide options for Executive Functions" is a UDL Guideline because it is a set of skills critical to academic success and is highly variable and context dependent.	
What do the UDL Guidelines say about executive functions?	The "Provide options for Self-Regulation" Guideline shares a row with the executive functions Guideline because they are strongly linked in a bidirectional feedback loop.	
How do teachers organize their thinking around executive functions?	Executive functions are developmental in nature (they improve over time as the brain develops), context dependent (the interaction between the learner and the environment plays a large role), and influenced by the body (e.g., fatigue can make it harder to use executive functions).	

PART II
Developing and Supporting Executive Functioning

In Part II, you'll find a collection of strategies and tools that will help you anticipate challenges your learners may face with executive functioning, as well as techniques that learners can use to recognize their own challenges and develop coping strategies for themselves. Many of these practical tips are rooted in the principles of UDL and intentionally chosen to be integrated into your learning environment so that learners feel empowered through easy-to-access supports and strategies.

The approaches offered here will strengthen the foundational skills that govern behaviors related to executive functioning. As with all foundations being built, however, you need to have scaffolding in place to support the process of anticipating executive functioning needs. You must also keep in mind that executive functions take time to develop and can be influenced by different factors. As these cognitive and emotional skills develop, the structure will become sturdier. With support and practice utilizing executive functions, learners will begin to strengthen the neural connections in their brain, and eventually these skills will become more automatic and habitual. Like a muscle that grows stronger with repeated exercise, intentional practice can lead to purposeful action. Given the relevance of executive functions to learning, on any given day, learners will benefit from having access to scaffolds for executive functioning. In fact, using many or all of these strategies yourself may support your own work and navigation through the school day. Whatever your reason for integrating executive functioning supports into your day-to-day experience, you will be setting a helpful and powerful example for your students. You can be explicit in reflecting to your students how executive functioning supports benefit you, even as an adult.

When we refer to learning environments, we mean any environment in which learning is the intended goal. This may be a physical classroom, a digital environment, or any other space where the intended goal is to explore, practice, and learn new content to acquire knowledge and skills. Though many different environments can provide opportunities to learn, it's important to design learning environments that provide *accessible, flexible, and facilitated* learning opportunities. For the purposes of this text, the strategies detailed here can be applied across the life span for early childhood, elementary, adolescent, young adult, and adult learners. Each strategy bolsters and supports executive functioning and aligns with the set of skills described in the UDL Guidelines—specifically, those that support executive functioning within the strategic network, with some overlap into the self-regulation Guidelines within the engagement network.

Since we can anticipate that there will be variability among executive functioning skills in any given learning environment, the goal is to embed scaffolds seamlessly so that students won't be able to tell the difference between a learner designated to have required supports (e.g., a 504 plan) and those who simply benefit from them: (i.e., all students).

These scaffolds and supports provide options for setting, planning for, and monitoring goals; receiving and integrating feedback; organizing information and resources to establish a clear plan; and addressing other avenues of establishing the foundations for purposeful learning. When we proactively consider and support executive functioning skills, we acknowledge how important it is to focus on the process of learning, rather than just an outcome. Providing options for navigating learning explorations where new information is being accessed and perceived (i.e., the UDL Guideline for providing multiple means of representation options for perception) is the starting point of task initiation. Over time, as you continue to find ways of scaffolding and supporting executive functions in your learning environment, you may begin to think about this process more intuitively. The scaffolding and support that you integrate to bolster executive functioning may eventually become an implicit "way of learning" rather than a perceived external resource or add-on.

The same will also be true for learners, who will gradually access supports for executive functioning as naturally as they access a writing tool or piece of technology to aid in their learning. With practice and over time, we want learners to utilize different skills to be able to inhibit inappropriate behaviors, hold on to new information, and think flexibly—the three foundational executive functioning skills. While there may be supports available to them, we also want learners to practice strengthening this set of cognitive skills more independently.

Think about learning a new game. You may need to read through the directions several times or refer to them regularly when you first start playing. This ensures that you're following the rules and everyone is playing by the same set of guiding principles. Over time, these rules become internalized. Players may occasionally refer to the rules as a refresher, but they can navigate them independently.

We want to acknowledge that there may be different ways to accomplish the same goal of supporting executive functioning. Suggestions we share may not be the only ways to integrate supports into your learning environment. We approach these strategies through the lens of the UDL framework, specifically its Guideline to support executive functioning by providing options for enhancing action and expression and for how students demonstrate their learning while setting themselves up to focus on the process and working toward learning goals. Ultimately, as educators we have the advantage of designing learning environments to promote strategic learning that enhances students' experiences. Flexibility, which is inherent to the UDL Guidelines and framework, reminds us there is no "one size fits all" approach to teaching or learning. And not only do we offer options and supports for students, but we also view the educators reading this book as learners who may benefit from scaffolds and supports as you begin to place executive functioning at the forefront of your designing and planning. We hope our examples, anecdotes, and the companion website will help support you on your journey.

5

ESTABLISHING CLEAR GOALS

How do we know where we're headed if we don't have a clear path established? Without specific goals, it's difficult to begin a journey. The possible scenarios that learners may be starting from, coupled with their previous experiences, can impact their current situation. In some cases, their approach to learning and work may be so automatic that they don't think much about how to learn something new or get something done. Other times, the path to reach a goal is dictated to them; they are told the exact directions to follow. And in some instances they must chart their own course, even if they don't have a clear sense of the best path forward. Each situation creates conditions that can cause uncertainty and thus impact executive functioning. Without clear goals, students may revert to unhelpful habits or approaches to learning or task completion that leave them confused and lost. When they don't know what to do to get started, they may stop completely in their tracks, unable to begin. Establishing clear goals with flexible means is a core UDL principle and the foundation to supporting executive functioning in learning. Clear goals allow learners across the life span to focus their efforts, establish a clear path with flexible options, and determine what they need to work toward and accomplish those goals.

> Most of the time I get an assignment and I don't know how to get started... it totally throws me off. A lot of times the teacher doesn't always give us enough information to know what they expect us to do. Like, "write this essay" does not always give me enough information to know what to do. Getting started is always the hardest part.
> —HIGH SCHOOL STUDENT

When learners hit a "stuck point" where they are uncertain about what is expected or how to get started, it's easy for them to fall into an all-or-nothing mentality. Ideally, we want learners to demonstrate inhibitory control and pause to assess what's needed as they are working toward any goal. At this point, resources, options, and alternative planning should be available to help them pivot from that stuck point to choose an alternate, more straightforward path. However, learners with developing executive functions may not feel confident enough with the skills and options they perceive to be available to pave a new path. This is when they can fall into the all-or-nothing mentality known in psychology as a *cognitive thinking trap*. When learners enter this mindset, they may have inner narratives or defensive responses like "I don't know what to do; it's not my fault!" or "Well, I had a plan, and it didn't work, so why even try again?" or "It's too late to start anyway." Oftentimes, a defensive response may aim to deflect attention from what they're struggling with to something else. When there is a lack of clarity in a goal, a fear of not doing well, or procrastination that leaves insufficient time to finish an assignment or task, learners may shut down and not complete their work at all—thereby landing on the "nothing" end of the all-or-nothing spectrum and not fulfilling their expected responsibilities. When the process of completing a task is stifled, it's often related to not being able to activate the executive functioning skills to get started.

Another reason why learners can have difficulty getting started is being unsure of what options are available or having too many options to choose from. A related behavior, which is closely linked to executive functioning, is organization. When too much information or choice is presented, it may be difficult for those with vulnerable executive functioning skills to organize what is available to them. Disorganization can further manifest in an all-or-nothing mindset, as it may feel dysregulating for those being affected by the experience. In these situations, learners who report feeling very overwhelmed when there are too many options, or when the one option they're presented with or that they try doesn't work the way they want it to, can become extremely rigid in their thinking. This can reinforce the stuck point and thus prevent them from getting started.

Even when there are other options available, having too many can leave a learner feeling overwhelmed. This may present as cognitive inflexibility, which can impede their ability to see beyond extreme options and leave them feeling hopeless rather than seeking assistance. In these examples, there may be a cognitive distortion where their brain is telling them there are no other options or ways forward, even when alternative paths are available. When the prefrontal cortex is developing or under stress related to trauma, anxiety, lack of resources, or overstimulation from the environment, people can be more vulnerable to all-or-nothing thinking. Considering the potential situations that may occur, and recognizing that each learner is showing up with a set of experiences and vulnerabilities, can help us remember to be clear with the goals we set in learning environments.

For learners with a vulnerable set of executive functioning skills, another way in which all-or-nothing thinking may show up is in perfectionistic tendencies. We may not think of perfectionist learners as lacking skills. Oftentimes, they have advanced skill sets in some domains, but when it comes to executive functioning skill activation, these cognitive skills may not be fully developed or may be influenced by the limbic system and emotionality. When students care deeply about an outcome, want to do their best, or hold themselves or their work to a high standard, they can also get stuck or have trouble initiating a task. Regardless of what they're capable of achieving or what they may have accomplished in the past, students exhibiting perfectionist tendencies often benefit from additional assistance to clarify goals, pace themselves, establish checkpoints for progress monitoring, and identify where they may be stuck.

Learners we have worked with across the life span have reported to us that when their work is not up to their own standards of "perfection," it often causes them to procrastinate. Upon reflection, such learners recognize that they were self-sabotaging by waiting until the last minute, then rushing through the task to complete and turn it in, if they do at all. In the end, they may justify their subpar performance by telling themselves they did not have enough time to do it well. In other words, they may compensate for the stress of not living up to their own potential by acting unconcerned about their lack of effort and focusing on not having enough time versus lacking skills. But in fact, these learners often report having a deep desire to have done better. This behavior of becoming incredibly stressed about a task or assignment, then waiting until the last minute to complete and turn it in, can often become a reinforced habit. When students score "well enough," they may continue along this path and, rather than becoming more strategic to minimize stress and increase the activation of skills to plan, organize, and efficiently execute a task, they limit the development of their executive functioning skills. Without practicing new approaches or skills and honest self-reflection, students engaged in this cycle can exacerbate the stress they feel when taking on new and complex tasks. Having clear goals can ameliorate and proactively address the all-or-nothing thinking and perfectionistic tendencies that can set this cycle into motion.

Similarly, reassurance seeking can limit the development of more strategic skills related to executive functioning. When learners check, double-check, or triple-check with their teachers that they're doing something correctly because they lack confidence in their skills, it limits their ability to develop and practice those skills independently. Younger students may not always be articulate in describing their experiences and may frequently seek reassurance from peers, trusted adults, or teachers to see how they are doing. This behavior can be avoidant, too, but is more often tied to a fear of making a mistake than to figuring out what needs to be improved. As the UDL Guidelines aim to develop expert learners, we want to provide options for learners to practice and work toward more independent skill development instead of relying only on external feedback. We want to encourage them to see errors or mistakes as opportunities to learn. When supporting the development of executive functioning, keep in mind that we want to scaffold the independent use of skills where students have supports to check in with and eventually have the opportunity to practice, make mistakes, and obtain feedback from others or through reflection to learn and grow their skills. The more opportunities they have to refine their approach, the more likely the all-or-nothing thinking, perfectionist tendencies, and reassurance seeking will dissipate so that strategic skill development can be maximized and integrated into learning and life.

> Perfectionism is like the ocean, it can ebb and flow, then completely knock you down making it hard for you to get back up. For me, it gets in my way of work. Sometimes I am able to think past it when I know clear small steps that I can achieve, but sometimes not.
>
> —SIXTH-GRADE STUDENT

Helping Learners Get Started

All students benefit from establishing clear goals. Can we help students determine a best place to start? Absolutely! Ideally, we can scaffold that first—and often most difficult—step of initiating tasks. Establishing clear goals with flexible means to reach them doesn't always come naturally and may take some practice to build confidence in creating them.

When designing learning opportunities, UDL reminds us to provide guidance on how to set goals that are clear, flexible, and rigorous. To support strategic thinking, it is helpful to model and scaffold how to set, establish, and map out a path toward learning goals. From these goals, educators can integrate graduated levels of support as needed as well as tangible ways for students to measure their own progress. Eventually, learners will integrate the skill of crafting and working toward a clear goal for themselves.

To check whether your goal meets those criteria, here are a few helpful questions that can guide your process (see Figure 5.1):

- Do students know what they are working toward?

- Do they know what is expected of them?

UDL Goal	UDL Goal
Clear Flexible Rigorous <u>Consider options for:</u> • Flexible means/paths to reach the goal • Graduated levels of scaffolds and support • Student-friendly language • Clear and concise goals • Visible learning outcomes	<u>Check:</u> It is clear that students know: What they're working toward? What is expected of them? There are different options to reach the goal? **Educators will:** • Use student-friendly language • Articulate goals clearly and concisely • Consider barriers and provide options to navigate around or through barriers

FIGURE 5.1. UDL goal-setting checklist and tips

- Are there different options available for students to access or reach the goal?

- Will students be able to map out a path to monitor their own progress with concrete checkpoints to see how they're doing along the way?

Designing the Planning Phase

Whenever you're establishing a goal students will work toward, we suggest integrating a planning phase as a part of that process. Students will map out their plan for how to complete each project or assignment that requires multiple steps. Oftentimes, teachers will set up these timelines and outlines for bigger projects; this planning phase also serves as a scaffold that gets folded into the assignment itself and will eventually become part of how a student's progress is assessed:

- Did the students establish a list of what is needed?

- Do they have helpful questions they are aiming to answer?

- Is there a timeline for what needs to happen first, next, and last?

- How long will each step take to complete?

- How will students know if they are progressing efficiently? Are there different checkpoints built in to monitor their progress?

For any learning activity where a student receives feedback or earns points for its completion, consider making this award for mapping out and executing steps part of their plans. When educators prioritize the process as an important part of the work, we shift students' focus to the steps to complete rather than just the final product. Criteria for utilizing executive functioning skills and related behaviors can be incorporated into a rubric to showcase how students considered and completed different phases of their work. You might provide some examples that show them how to clarify the goal, establish a plan with checkpoints to monitor progress, and demonstrate what "complete" looks like. Engaging students in this process also provides an opportunity for them to brainstorm what resources and assistance they may need. When learners pause to reflect and confirm what they know and have available, they can proactively plan and prepare before beginning a task. Doing so can disrupt patterns of rigidity or all-or-nothing thinking.

Students can showcase their skills in different ways. They could prepare a proposal of what they intend to do for the project with a plan of measurable checkpoints leading to their goal, create a video or audio tutorial describing the steps and stages of the project, or create some other tool to demonstrate their plan.

Encouraging Self-Reflection and Feedback

Incorporating predictable opportunities for reflection and feedback provides guidance for learners to develop a better understanding of how they are doing and to check in before turning in completed work. Using a rubric of expected criteria is another way for students to check in about how they're doing as they strive to reach their goals. Ideally, student and teacher ratings can be embedded into the rubric so that students can contribute reflections on their process and compare their own ratings to those of their teacher. The more we can scaffold, encourage, and support progress monitoring, the better. Doing so promotes not only reflection but also cognitive flexibility as learners pause to assess how they are doing and what they can improve.

Rather than telling learners what to do (e.g., "you need to be more flexible"), we want to encourage and strengthen their decision-making skills. One of the mindset shifts that we teach learners is to consider the goal of each endeavor, point of learning, discussion, or opportunity to self-advocate. No matter the situation, taking a moment to pause and think about what the goal is can make a big difference.

Rather than getting stuck in a fixed mindset, we want students to consider what Carol Dweck (2006) and colleagues call a *growth mindset*. When we think flexibly about a situation so we can see different paths to or perspectives on a goal, we are activating cognitive flexibility. As students consider the question, "What's the goal?" they have the opportunity to evaluate their level of clarity around what they're working on and toward. When learners understand the relevance of clear goals and planning (which supports their engagement in their own learning), their experience transforms from viewing a project as simply a task or assignment they need to complete to appreciating the importance of the process.

Asking the simple question, "What's the goal?" encourages learners to think strategically and better plan all that they do. This one question can provide additional context and guidance for how students communicate, organize, plan, and prioritize in all aspects of their lives.

Being clear about goals can break down barriers. Why do we make the decisions we do? We've heard many stories from learners about how they were prevented access to an accommodation, assistive technology, or other flexible options that would have built a stronger bridge from where they were to their end target. One example is from a middle-school student who left his calculator at home and needed it to graph quadratics for a quiz. The teacher, rather than lending his own calculator to this student, created a barrier for—and some would say punished—the student by saying, "You should have remembered to bring yours."

In this moment, what was the teacher's goal? Was he trying to prove a point, teach a lesson, or assess this student's math abilities through the assessment? Whatever the goal, the outcome was that the student became embarrassed and frustrated. In fact, this one interaction led to countless struggles for the student in his math studies that year, as he was disengaged due to his teacher not supporting his efforts and needs. The lack of trust in his teacher led to some precarious future interactions, and it took quite a while to repair his engagement in the process of learning, despite his enjoying math challenges and wanting to do well. How could this have gone differently?

In our opinion, this could have been a great opportunity to get curious. The teachable lesson here is not "Got ya—you should've had the calculator to be successful today!" but the importance of asking, "How can we make adjustments so you're better prepared next time?" Could that teacher have taken a moment to ask, "What do you think got in the way of you bringing your calculator to school today?" The difference in response to this situation would have shifted the goal from punishment to curiosity. When we take the time to create a teachable moment, the student is prompted to think about what they could have done differently and what they could do differently in the future. Considering the goal for these types of interactions when giving feedback and making instructional choices may take a few extra moments, but ultimately can shift a potentially disengaging situation into a learning experience.

Intentionality is key. Asking one simple question, "What's the goal?" can create respectful, safe, and supportive learning environments that prioritize learning, curiosity, and exploration to maximize equity.

SMART Goals

One tool that helps students focus on the process of learning and doing—especially to establish clarity in goals, map out a plan, and create checkpoints to monitor progress and promote

Using Points as Feedback

In a few instances we've alluded to awarding points as a tool for assessing or supporting learner work. We aren't taking a stance for or against using a numerical system for this purpose; rather, we want to emphasize that the points attributed to any work are arbitrary if we're not focusing on the process of student learning, planning, practice, execution, and reflection (i.e., the parts of the learning process that can strengthen executive functions). When we provide specific feedback, praise process-oriented learning, and de-emphasize the importance of the end product, learners may become more in tune with their own learning to become strategic learners, rather than just going through the motions or working for points or grades. We want to encourage the process, not just the outcome.

accountability—is the SMART mnemonic, which stands for specific, measurable, attainable, relevant, and timely. This tool not only serves to establish clear goals and provides a framework to check effective goal setting but also builds awareness of what is needed, what is possible, and what helps. In reality, students won't likely fill out or establish SMART goals for every learning task they begin; however, building this tool into assignments allows them to pause and check themselves to ensure they're clear about their goals. It can even become a fixture at the beginning of any task or assignment. As educators, we can model what these goals look like, and later students can fill in what is specific, measurable, attainable, relevant, and timely for each task they complete. Mapping out their plan and determining each step and stage this way helps students establish accountability.

We often hear students say, "My goal is to do better in school" or "I want to get all As." These might seem like reasonable goals and could even make an adult or two in their lives gush with pride; however, they can reflect an all-or-nothing mindset. Educators can help the learner add nuance to their goals by asking what "do better" means. The answer might look different to different students or at different points in time. We can push the line of questioning even further to ask what it will look like when the student is "doing better in school" and how they themselves or others will know when they've reached this goal. Engaging in genuinely curious, supportive conversations (without judgment, as silly as some goals may seem!) stimulates reflection that can lead to deep, creative thinking and learning.

When we engage learners in deep, specific, and timely reflection, we often see an increase in motivation, leading to skill mastery and a greater sense of agency to map their own paths and seek the resources and assistance they need while working toward their goals.

Ultimately, we want learners to consider SMART goals as guides or signposts to assist in their planning to reach a goal. In Figure 5.2, the questions below each word guide learners to be clear about the specific goal; how it will be measured; and if it is attainable, relevant, and timely. This is especially important for *backward planning*—establishing an end date and working backward to set guideposts for

ESTABLISH CLEAR GOALS THAT ARE

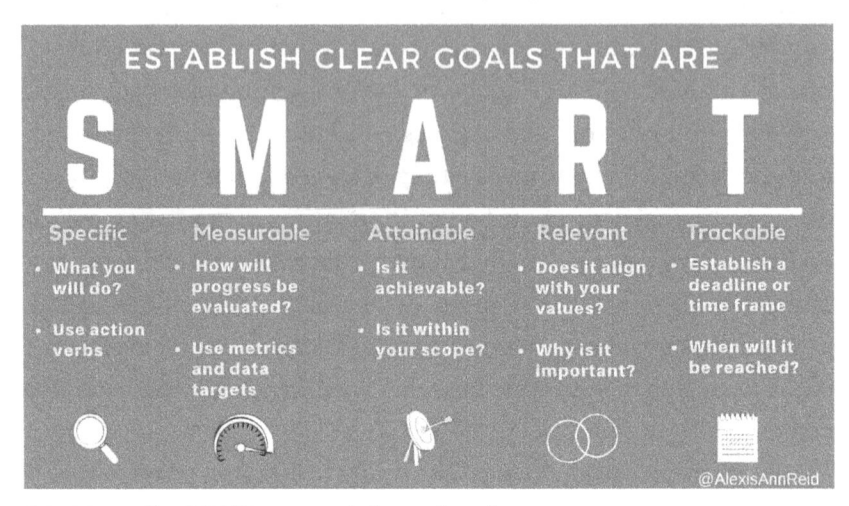

S M A R T

Specific	Measurable	Attainable	Relevant	Trackable
• What you will do? • Use action verbs	• How will progress be evaluated? • Use metrics and data targets	• Is it achievable? • Is it within your scope?	• Does it align with your values? • Why is it important?	• Establish a deadline or time frame • When will it be reached?

@AlexisAnnReid

FIGURE 5.2. The SMART mnemonic for goal setting

different stages of the process. Many students have difficulty budgeting enough time to get started, do the work, and check before completing it. When following SMART goals, they can assess whether the goal is even an appropriate and attainable challenge to take on right now (considering the context); consider whether it's relevant, important to them and their learning journey, and timely; and establish some endpoint. Again, the goal is to think about what is needed, what is helpful, and how progress will be measured.

What Helps:

- **Share your why.** If you want learners to practice using a specific tool, strategy, or approach, share that with them. We want to shift away from emphasizing compliance as a form of engagement in the classroom and instead encourage learners to explore, co-create, and expand their knowledge through experiences. When we share our process—our *why* for what we do in learning environments—it targets the UDL principle of providing multiple means of engagement. It also helps to activate the strategic network as executive functions begin to come online.

- **Be explicit.** Remember that students aren't coming from your same context, background, or experience. We want to meet learners where they are or help bring them closer to what we share with them. Use clear, explicit examples and describe the components of the goal to show how it helps to have a clear target to aim for while learning and working. Why is this important to you, and how will it help?

    For example: "For this lesson we are aiming to understand decimal concepts as related to dollars and cents by exploring up to the hundredths place value. This will help us with buying things and making change."

- **Set the stage** about what your goals are in a lesson to set the stage for learners to establish SMART goals for themselves.

Start out a unit or larger project with an exercise for students to map out their own SMART goal for their work. What are they aiming for? Is it in line with the curricular goals? How will they measure or monitor how they are doing? Who will assist them along the way? Can they extend their current thinking to use concepts in real-world scenarios? Will they ask for assistance or additional guidance to expand their thinking and learning? All of these should be encouraged in a learning environment whenever possible.

- **Activate prior knowledge and curiosity** by starting with a topic or concept and having students share what they already know about it. This can become a web of ideas on a board, sticky notes around the topic, or some other digital representation of each student's contribution. These webs can become a great starting point to establish a plan for research, helpful questions, or checkpoints to guide the process along the way (see Figure 5.3).

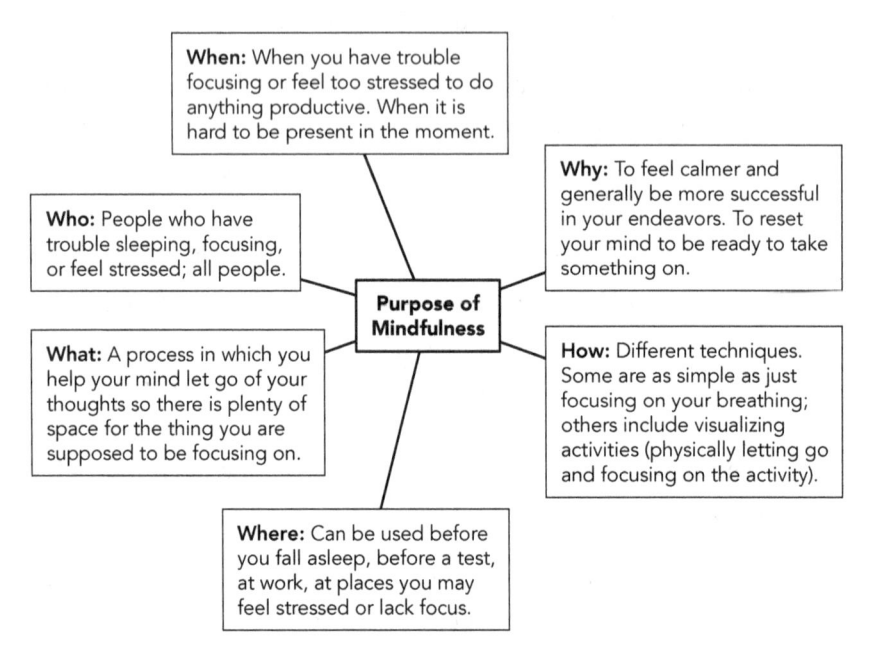

Purpose of Mindfulness

When: When you have trouble focusing or feel too stressed to do anything productive. When it is hard to be present in the moment.

Why: To feel calmer and generally be more successful in your endeavors. To reset your mind to be ready to take something on.

Who: People who have trouble sleeping, focusing, or feel stressed; all people.

What: A process in which you help your mind let go of your thoughts so there is plenty of space for the thing you are supposed to be focusing on.

How: Different techniques. Some are as simple as just focusing on your breathing; others include visualizing activities (physically letting go and focusing on the activity).

Where: Can be used before you fall asleep, before a test, at work, at places you may feel stressed or lack focus.

FIGURE 5.3. Brainstorming ideas created by a fifth-grade student

Establishing SMART goals takes time and practice. When in doubt, ask your students what they may be unclear about or what else they would like to know as they plan their process for working toward goals. Encouraging an inquiry process is essential to facilitating strategic thinking and learning. An established clear goal can be broken down into smaller parts and steps to devise a path to follow.

Whenever possible, scaffold students to better assess the accuracy of their SMART goals, especially how much time it might take for them to complete any part of a task (see Figure 5.4).

SMART GOALS

Specific (What exactly do I want to accomplish?)

Measurable (How will I know when my goal is met?)

Attainable (Is that a realistic goal that I can reach?)

Relevant (How will meeting this goal help me?)

Timely (When will I accomplish this goal?)

My Goal:

Target date to reach my goal:

This goal is important to me because:

Potential barriers to be mindful of:

Who are the people, places or resources that can help to reach this goal?

If I get stuck I can reach out to _____ and ask for _____.

I will check in with _____ after I have completed checkpoint(s) _____.

I will set myself up for success by:

What do I need to start doing, do differently, or keep doing to achieve this goal?

How: Map out steps to achieve the goal

Step	Looks like (I need . . .)	Potential distractors to be mindful of	Deadline

Other reminders that may be helpful:

FIGURE 5.4. SMART Goals worksheet

Have students start with one task and time how long it might take to complete it to help determine metrics and measure progress, and hold themselves accountable along the way (see Figure 5.5).

	Estimated time	Actual time to complete	Additional notes
How long did it take to ...			
Determine the first two steps to begin			
Brainstorm and map out a plan			

FIGURE 5.5. Time tracker

Sometimes goals are dictated by a curriculum, and other times they're established by an educator or student, but either way, they're usually composed of multiple levels and layers that students are working toward. We want to be mindful of what we're communicating when we work on goals with our students. It's helpful to share our own goals, motivations, and overall planning approach in different situations. When we are vulnerable with students in this way, it often helps them recognize that everyone benefits from supports, reminders, and breaks.

KEY TAKEAWAYS FROM CHAPTER 5

	CHAPTER SUMMARY	YOUR NOTES
Why should we proactively support executive functioning in learning environments?	When we are clear about goals, we can empower learners to take control of the way they navigate learning new content, showing what they know, and transforming their knowledge into meaningful explorations that practice and support executive functioning development.	
What are the best approaches to supporting learners' executive functioning?	Have students break down the component parts of assignments, projects, or new content being learned. We want to meet students where they are by activating prior knowledge, helping them determine the relevance of the work, and enabling autonomy by clearly conveying what is expected of them. SMART goals focus on the process of acquiring and using new knowledge. When we provide resources and explicitly practice how to access and determine what is possible, we are teaching not just content but skills that will last a lifetime.	
How do I get started?	Make what is often implicit and kept in our heads more explicit. Help learners understand what the goals are and that the process is just as important as the outcome. Practice establishing clear goals, have students map out SMART goals, make time more visible, and make these often difficult strategies and skills more fun to use and accessible.	

6

DETERMINING PRIORITIES AND CREATING A PLAN

Even with clearly established goals, it can be challenging for students to prioritize tasks by importance because their executive functions are still developing. Sometimes learners may prioritize completing less important tasks rather than engage in those that require deeper thinking or more time to complete. This becomes particularly apparent for learners who have multiple assignments or responsibilities at the same time. In these situations, you can help learners understand how to set priorities in different ways. First, before we support student academic goals, we need to recognize that there's often an emotional component to determining what takes priority. Most of the time, students don't recognize the systems, dynamics, or reasoning taking place when they're prioritizing what needs their attention. If they're hungry, their priority may be to hunt down a snack; if they're socially driven, they may focus on staying connected to their classmates instead of doing the work at hand. Being able to demonstrate inhibitory control and focus their attention while regulating their physiological and emotional systems is an important foundation for learning how to manage priorities. Without this foundation established, we may see irregular or random approaches to learning. We can support learners in prioritizing so they become more intentional and strategic learners.

Providing support for prioritizing is not without its own barriers, however. Prioritizing where to focus resources like effort, attention, and time on task is emotional work. For learners with developing executive functions, one of the greatest challenges is determining what is most important. Not knowing what's important or where to start can cause insecurity, and learners may begin to second-guess themselves or feel as though they should be able to figure out what to do on their own. As students have more and more experiences of struggling to prioritize their work or determine how to get started, they may begin to "should" all over themselves and develop negative self-talk, which can diminish confidence. Rather than ask for assistance, they may retreat to other behaviors.

When we as teachers notice students who are struggling to prioritize how to use their resources, we can intervene to help guide their process. The skill of prioritization often takes time, patience, guidance, and practice. These skills get strengthened through modeling, practice, and feedback across contexts. What someone believes is important in one context at a given moment or time may be different than what someone else thinks. As educators we can be clear about our goals and expectations so that learners are able to establish a plan with smaller steps to reach those goals. From there, they can use the sequence of steps or deadlines to determine where to begin. When we provide multiple means of action and expression to emphasize the importance of the planning stage of the process, it reinforces the skill of prioritization.

What Helps:
- **Use a rubric** to establish expectations.

Rubrics are used far and wide these days, but *how* we use them matters. We can shift their purpose from a way to assess student work to a way to establish how students navigate their work.

Promoting strategic learning to support executive functioning skills starts with how we design and implement tools such as rubrics. Well-designed rubrics clearly describe expectations by providing criteria and checkpoints for learners to establish a plan and show what they know. Prior to turning in an assignment, learners can use a rubric to reflect on their work and make adjustments as needed to improve it. This step in the process can be built into the assignment or goal. The typical approach is to tell students that something is due by a certain date. These deadlines are often helpful to limit the amount of time students spend on any one task. As suggested in the previous chapter, it can be helpful to build in a part of the process where students map out how much time they estimate is needed to complete each part of their plan. This shift in approach establishes checkpoints for students to fill out their rubrics and reflect on the work they have or haven't yet completed. These reflections can provide greater insight about a student's process and decision making, as well as an opportunity to offer suggestions, feedback, and intervention *during* the process of learning and creating rather than at the end. Doing so can help guide students later as they're prioritizing different portions of bigger or longer-term projects and assignments.

If you need a score for record-keeping and grading purposes, the rubric can become a score card for students to use. With their individual ratings alongside the teacher ratings on the rubric, students can compare the scores they gave themselves to those you've awarded them. Once students share their reflections, you may choose to average the students' self-scores with your own ratings. An additional feedback section can allow students to share how they got to the final product they submitted. Learners can then pause to reflect on how they accomplished their goal through multiple modalities—text, audio or video, a visualization, or another creative medium of expressing themselves. Students can share any barriers they faced, as well as ideas about what they'd do differently in the future. Regardless of how reflection and planning is integrated into an assignment, each part of the process should be as valuable as the final product.

Table 6.1 is a sample rubric for a book review focused on the process rather than just the outcome.

What Does Finished Look Like?

One exercise to help students prioritize the work they aim to accomplish is to map out what different levels of being finished can mean or look like. Doing so can help them release concerns stemming from uncertainty or perfectionistic tendencies. Oftentimes, assignments are given and students immediately assume all of them have equal value and importance, when in reality teachers often assign work for exploration, practice, extension, or other purposes. Setting expectations and levels of completion can break down tasks into specific skills or components, equipping students to engage in more purposeful prioritizing to determine how to complete tasks efficiently.

TABLE 6.1. A Process-Focused Book Review Rubric

Goal: Demonstrate your understanding of the independent reading book you completed.		0 = Please revisit 1 = Approaching 2 = Achieved		
Element	**Description**	**0**	**1**	**2**
Planning	• Created a plan with checkpoints to monitor progress (at least three were mapped out). • Checked back to determine timing and pacing of work getting completed and asked for feedback to assess what else is needed. • Reached out for assistance or asked for feedback as needed. Notes:			
Characters	• Described the main characters in the book, their traits, and how and why they change over the course of the book. Notes:			
Story elements	• Included a clear summary and overview of the primary story elements* within the book, including setting, problem, and solution. * See story map graphic organizer. Notes:			
Theme	• Provided a discussion of ideas about the theme (life lesson) or central message of the story, with evidence from the text and analysis of the importance of the evidence to support each point made. Notes:			
Creativity and clarity	• Project incorporated original ideas and creative elements to establish an engaging final product. • Elements used and descriptions were clear as well as easy to follow and understand. Notes:			
Timing and reflection	• Process to complete this project included checkpoints to see if progress was on track. • If a different approach was needed, the plan and timeline were adjusted. • Timeline was followed or conferencing occurred to get back on track. • Final reflection was thoughtfully completed. Notes:			
Total: **Identified barriers:** **Points for improvement:**				

Table 6.2 is an example of a guide learners can use to assess their work and determine what level of completion is required, and thus how much time, energy, and focus they need to work toward that goal. When developing strategic learning skills, we want to help students demonstrate inhibitory control, prioritize their efforts while thinking flexibility about how to create a plan, and work mindfully toward their goals. Learners developing executive functioning skills may focus their time on more familiar, less challenging tasks or overdo tasks or skills they have already mastered. Setting expectations before they get started enables students to map a path that is reasonable for them. Sometimes they've already practiced specific skills enough, so they can shift or move on to their next level, task, or learning goal. This may be challenging for some, as they're still strengthening their cognitive flexibility and ability to switch from one task or goal to another.

Ultimately, we want learners to shift from focusing on the volume of the work they need to complete or just getting things done to focusing on the process or path they take to learn. As we've discussed, this happens by reflecting on what and how they need to prioritize to successfully work toward their goals.

As a middle-grade student explained: "I know that I have all of these assignments to do, but it usually takes me hours each night to get through them. Okay, maybe I am not always as focused as I need to be on each assignment when I am 'doing homework,' but it always just seems like it will take so much time. What I figured out is that sometimes I don't always need to 'overdo' things and can just get through them so that I can dedicate more of my energy on the tougher assignments. I ended up creating a system to think about how much time and effort I need to complete different assignments to help me plan out my day."

TABLE 6.2. Categorization of Expectations

ASSIGNMENT	MINIMUM TO BE FINISHED	WELL DONE	EXTREME VERSION
Plan and compose one paragraph about the purpose of mindfulness.	• Topic sentence • Three ideas • Conclusion	• Has a flow, gets the point across, and has some good vocabulary • Topic sentence • Three ideas • Conclusion	• Topic sentence, plus at least three details to support the topic and analysis/expansion of ideas • Conclusion (paraphrase topic sentence/takeaway) • Strong details that are related to the topic • Sophisticated vocabulary • Good flow of ideas—maintains theme • Includes good sources

You can complete the extreme version . . . but at what expense will it get done at that level?

Be mindful of finding balance and monitoring the resources you need to use to complete all your responsibilities and take care of you.

Aim for quality over quantity!

Prioritization and Working Memory

How students prioritize what they need to do can be influenced by various motivations and distractions. At any given moment, there's only so much information anyone can take in and learn. Different stressors or distractions may be competing for student attention or focus, limiting their capacity to take in new information. This capacity is sometimes referred to as *cognitive load* (Sweller, 2011). Even students who are highly engaged can find it challenging to retain information or discern what's relevant if too much is presented at one time. Presenting too much information can tax learners' working memory and cause them to miss important pieces of information. The ability to organize and prioritize the most important information and tasks is a higher-order skill that develops with instruction, practice, experience, and time.

As one sixth-grade student said: "My teachers give me so many different assignments every day and I never think I can finish them on time. For homework, I usually have different assignments that I sometimes write down in my planner, but other times I need to find online. Either way, it all just feels like too much and I don't know what is the most important to start with. Every morning I have a big packet that I am supposed to be working on, but my brain isn't even turned on yet, let alone able to get through all of that work first thing in the morning."

When learners take too long to get started or complete a task, it may be because they're unsure how to prioritize their time and efforts. This can translate to well-intentioned individuals around them (helpful peers, adults, caregivers) swooping in to prioritize or organize for them to save time or get them through to the next step or stage. Although we want to recognize and validate each learner's unique needs and may prioritize information, tasks, and resources in different ways, you can best support their executive functioning skills by helping them figure out how to handle the trouble they're having prioritizing tasks. For example, a student may plan to complete classwork "later" for homework, but they may not recognize that doing so could compromise their downtime before bed or their ability to complete more urgent assignments by their due date. By pointing out the consequences or the longer-term goals that their short-term decisions may be affecting, you can help them learn to reframe their priorities and take ownership of their decisions.

One example, an excerpt of which is shown in Table 6.3, is from a middle-school student who created a way to keep track of her assignments using Google Docs.

TABLE 6.3. A Student-Created Agenda for Prioritizing Assignments

Steps to Start
- First we list out all that needs to get done.
- Then, consider the urgency of each assignment based on due dates.
- Prioritize what to complete first and thereafter.
- Establish times and due dates for each assignment in parentheses.

Key:
Green: Basic assignment (quick, usually due next day)
Yellow: Requires more energy/focus
Red: Difficult project (requires focus and most resources)
Gray: Recurring each week

Green and yellow assignments should be completed after school. Red and gray assignments are ideally saved for the weekend.

	Math	Social Studies	ELA	Science	Music Practice/Other
Monday					
Tuesday					
Wednesday					
Thursday					
Friday					
Weekend					

Notice the steps to set up this agenda and the color-coded key (although you'll have to use your imagination since the book is printed in black and white!). Not only is she listing out what she needs to get done for classes each day, but she is also assigning a level of effort and focus needed for each assignment. This allows her to prioritize her assignments based on how much energy and focus she needs to complete them, which in turn helps her prioritize how much time she should spend on each task so she can schedule her homework efforts accordingly. Similar tools can be established for younger or older students, with differences across developmental levels based on how much scaffolding, time to fill in, and support is provided for learners to map out their plans.

Making Time to Collaborate

To emphasize the work you're asking students to do to prioritize their goals and assignments, ask them to share their plans. When students share their approaches and have open discourse about their planning, prioritization, and reasons for choosing a certain approach, they can learn about alternative ways of prioritizing. Oftentimes, it's less about using a specific tool, and more about reflecting on and discussing their choices and plans. When you encourage such activities, students are practicing to strengthen skills to solidify their approach. It also gives them time to slow down and check themselves as they further organize their plan or ask for suggestions before getting started. While prioritizing the information they need, resources that may be helpful, sequence of tasks to complete, and time they need to achieve their end goals, they're also practicing skills related to comprehension, providing evidence to support their ideas and choices, and thinking critically and holistically about their decisions. Prioritization can be scaffolded with prompts for thinking, guided support, and examples of "important information" that can be summarized at the end of a learning exploration, assignment, or reading.

Creating a Plan to Strengthen Working Memory Skills

Increasing learners' awareness of how they hold on to new information and do something with it in a timely manner helps to strengthen their working memory skills. Students often report that they're not retaining the information they're given, not turning in assignments, or not sure of what needs to get done—regardless of how clear and detailed our directions were. When we acknowledge that working memory can be influenced by many different factors in the environment and within oneself (remember, stress and anxiety can also affect the ability to hold information in mind), we can slow things down and help learners check in about what they need and what is next. In these moments, we can assess what may be the barrier to determine the variables at play. Helping learners determine which tools or approaches are most helpful to record assignments, steps, or tasks can anchor their attention and keep them on task, and creating a task list inherently strengthens working memory, as it's like a mental rehearsal of what they need to do to reach the goal at hand.

Even when educators post what needs to get done, it doesn't always ensure that the information will be understood or the steps will be carried out as intended. Take a few moments to have students make their own version of the directions or task list for what needs to get done. Give them the time and space to set their own agenda or steps to reach a goal in their own words and allow for a moment where they can check in with a classmate or teacher to be sure their plan makes sense before getting started. To reinforce the importance of this stage of the process, it can be weighted in a similar way to the final product.

We recommend making the planning for assignments a significant part of the feedback or score earned for the full completion of the assignment. Emphasizing how planning establishes the foundation for the work increases its value. Ultimately, these tools and strategies can become the beginning of the process. When we spend some extra time modeling, practicing, and supporting students' understanding of the learning process, we set them up for success and potentially reduce extra time needed for intervention or redirection. As their focus shifts to the process, learners also have an opportunity to develop skills that increase their independence and deepen their understanding of how they learn best.

It may seem like a simple strategy to have students establish a task list, agenda, planner, or app to help keep track of all that needs to get done. However, for many it doesn't seem like a natural solution. You'd probably be surprised to hear how many students we've worked with over the years refused to use a list or write things down, or even expressed a sense of pride that they can "hold on to information in their minds." The trick here is that our brains don't always have the capacity to hold on to too many pieces of information at a time.

Consider how a high school student describes their experience: "I would say something that helped me not only for academic purposes, but also my mental health, would be to write down . . . just the practice of like writing down all that I need to do. I think, definitely, in a world where assignments and stuff like that are all posted online, and you just see, an endless array of notifications, and it just goes to your head . . . I have a million things to do, I'm just going to push it aside. I think I've definitely learned how to do things in small steps. But that starts with getting it all out. And I think just that process can be very satisfying. And can feel like a bit of a release."

As we mentioned earlier, there's a reason that phone numbers, Social Security numbers, and even locker combinations are chunked into smaller parts: so that we can remember the information and be able to use it in some way. If the goal is to immediately use the information given, we can support that process. If, on the other hand, the goal is to store new information into long-term memory, there are ways to scaffold and support that process, too. We often assume that students can just remember the directions they're given. For younger learners, especially, it's important to break down and reinforce the delivery of information in multiple modalities. Think about the UDL Guideline for multiple means of representation. Can we provide and reinforce directions or instructions in multiple modalities that learners can access independently and repeatedly as needed? Or, can students also translate instructions in a way that makes sense to them?

It's important to be mindful of gradually releasing the scaffolds for the learner to build mastery in these skills independently. We want to find a balance between guiding the learner and the learner guiding themselves in identifying what they need. With that, it's also important to be cognizant of how adults or other learners can hinder this process—the more we do for students, the less they may be strengthening their own skills and independence.

What Helps:
- **Create checklists.** Sticky notes, notepads, checklists, and online digital apps are all options for creating some version of a task list. Work with students to determine which will be best to meet each individual's needs.

    Sometimes a simple sticky note can be more effective than trying to hold information in mind.

    Using larger sticky notes can be helpful to break down bigger tasks into smaller parts or to color-code and indicate when something needs to get finished. These can be color-coded to represent "Do Now," "Schedule," or "Do Later," like so (again, use your imagination to add color!):

DO NOW	SCHEDULE	DO LATER

Determining Priorities and Creating a Plan   91

If students already use technology for planning or scheduling, meet them where they are and have them practice integrating task lists or "to dos" into their digital planners or systems.

The key here is to practice with them. We may assume that since students use technology (especially as they get older) they know how to use digital tools. Often, that's not the case, and some explicit instruction and guided practice is beneficial.

If you're unsure what is needed, get curious and ask students to show what they currently use, ask how they currently use their calendaring/planning devices, and meet them where they are. By asking helpful questions, we can align with learners, more accurately assess what is needed, and appropriately scaffold and support them accordingly.

- **"When in doubt, chunk it out"** (Figure 6.1) is a catchy saying that focuses on the psychological terminology of "chunking" larger pieces of information into smaller bits or chunks.

FIGURE 6.1. Chunking information can make it easier to retain.

Remember that phone numbers and codes are often broken down into sets of three or four numerals, which is in line with storing information into short-term memory to encode it for immediate or future use. Chunking or batching allows for grouping information (ideally that's related in some way) into smaller, more manageable parts visually, auditorially, tactilely, or otherwise.

Be sure not to give too many steps or tasks at a time. If needed, chunk into shorter or fewer steps to support working memory skills.

- **Highlight critical components or information.** When creating a goal or introducing new information or learning explorations, begin or end your presentation by clearly defining critical features of each learning goal. Similar to how this book includes "key takeaways" at the end of each chapter along with questions to consider, highlighting the most helpful points guides students as they gain experience prioritizing the information they encounter.

    These key points, essential questions, objectives, critical questions to consider, or primary concepts to focus on while reading or learning can be labeled however you like, as long as they point to themes and information that should be prioritized.

- **Prioritize time and consider urgency.** The four-quadrant weekly plan from Stephen Covey's *Seven Habits of Highly Productive People* (1998) provides an example that can be used to support students' prioritization of what needs to be done with more or less urgency.

    Using this "time management" matrix helps us consider how we spend our time. Rather than "managing" our time, we can reflect on what is important to prioritize, what gets in the way, what can get delegated or wait until later, and what we can use to celebrate after completing important tasks. Being aware of how we prioritize and spend our time is crucial to determining how we can more effectively use it.

Students can use a matrix like the one shown in Figure 6.2 to assess what needs to get done and when, what could get in their way, and how they want to prioritize their resources, energy, and time for completing responsibilities. Have students use their own labels to make the table more relevant and engage them in the process.

	URGENT	NOT URGENT
IMPORTANT	**"Putting Out Fires"** **Do first** • Deadline-driven urgent projects • Pressing problems • Crises • Emergencies	**"Quality Time"** **Plan out and do on schedule** • Relationship building • Regular self-care • Planned tasks/work • Pursuing new opportunities
NOT IMPORTANT	**"Distractions"** **Delegate or use as breaks** • Interruptions and conversations • Some mail/calls/texts • Unscheduled meetings • Popular social activities	**"Time Wasters"** **Avoid or use to celebrate** • Trivial "busywork" • Some mail/calls/texts • Social media • Games and other non-urgent activities

Adapted from "The Time Management Matrix" by Stephen R. Covey (2004).

Do now/ASAP: ☐

Plan for the next few days (routines or schedules/habits to increase): ☐

To be mindful of or to celebrate with: ▪

FIGURE 6.2. Priorities matrix

- **Work with learners to determine the most effective prioritization tool for them.** In a "Top Priorities" to-do list like Figure 6.3, prompts are built in to help students consider what is needed, how much time it may take to complete, and how they worked toward their goals.

Date:			
Top priorities and steps to complete	Resources needed	Estimated time to complete	Performance rating
		Estimated: Actual:	Unfocused on task
		Estimated: Actual:	Unfocused on task
		Estimated: Actual:	Unfocused on task
		Estimated: Actual:	Unfocused on task

FIGURE 6.3. To-do list: Top priorities

KEY TAKEAWAYS FROM CHAPTER 6

	CHAPTER SUMMARY	YOUR NOTES
Why is scaffolding prioritization of resources, information, time, and effort so important?	Prioritizing information is often one of the most challenging tasks for learners. Depending on the context, importance of the task, and each learner's experience, they can prioritize very differently than an educator intends. These skills must be scaffolded so learners are able to assess what is most important in relation to the goal.	
What systems are influenced by an overabundance of information or lack of clarity?	Remember that cognitive load can be limited in situations where too much information or too many tasks are presented at once. Breaking information or instructions down into smaller parts, or "chunks," helps isolate smaller steps to make learning and completing tasks more manageable. Chunking can also provide clarity for students to better organize, manage, and prioritize tasks or steps to get started.	
How do I get started?	Consider how you already provide directions and assign projects as well as potential scaffolds to promote clarity and prioritization. Before shifting to students working independently, discuss and brainstorm ideas for what learners consider most important to get a sense of their thinking. Allow them to collaborate with their peers so they can hear different perspectives and map out a path that's in line with the goal. Taking an extra few minutes to allow for this work or conversation can increase the level, clarity, and organization of the learning and work they're engaged in.	

7

TEACHING METACOGNITION AND REFLECTION

Developing metacognition can strengthen a learner's ability to be strategic. *Metacognition* involves reflecting on a situation to think about your own thinking. When learners pause to reflect, they allow themselves time to determine what they need and how they learn best. By asking questions like "What do I need to complete this task?" or "How am I doing?" students are practicing inhibitory control, self-monitoring, and cognitive flexibility. When they activate metacognitive skills by inhibiting distracting behaviors to pause for reflection, learners can better understand how they learn across different contexts and time, which in turn helps them monitor progress and make decisions that support their own learning.

Metacognitive skills begin to come online in upper elementary and the middle years and develop throughout adolescence. As they develop, these skills require modeling, patience, time, and practice. For this reason, students learning how to be metacognitive often face some common initial challenges.

First, learners may not always be accurate evaluators of their own progress and process. As educators, we often recognize when students are struggling with concepts, social situations, or approaches to learning, but when students examine their situation themselves to determine what needs to be done, they may assess their skills inaccurately or face other factors that can impact performance. We've all seen a student chatting with a classmate, exhibiting distracting behavior, or trying to leave the classroom to avoid a perceived challenge. (We say "perceived" here because depending on the context, a task that normally could have been carried out may feel more difficult than usual if our systems are challenged differently.) These behaviors are typical human responses, but they may indicate a limitation or lack of metacognitive skill. If not approached from a place of curiosity, these learners may become rigid, defensive, or even more avoidant. In these moments we want to be mindful of not embarrassing and eliciting shame by calling out a learner for their behaviors, but instead asking helpful questions about their circumstances. Doing so helps learners build an awareness of their behaviors to prompt reflection and presents educators with a potential opportunity to guide, model, or support another path forward. These skills are precursors to activating and strengthening cognitive flexibility.

The antithesis of metacognition is staying stuck or rigid when faced with a perceived challenge, which is what most learners who are developing executive functioning skills tend to revert to. As an elementary student shared, "When I know I have something to do, it is not that I don't want to do it, sometimes I set myself up, motivated to get it done, and I just get stuck. I literally cannot move forward." In this instance, a teacher, peer, mentor, or coach can provide prompts to scaffold metacognition for the student to consider alternative options to the current situation. We want learners to be aware of the challenge and recognize that there's more than one path or option available to choose from—which is, again, the basis for cognitive flexibility.

Perceived challenge may not be the only time when it is difficult to access cognitive flexibility. Think about a time when you have been especially tired, stressed, or even misunderstood. These are often circumstances where we lack clarity and thus the flexibility to efficiently determine how to navigate changes and challenges that arise in our day-to-day lives. We want to capture and teach students of all ages what may be coming up for them in these situations. When learners build an awareness of triggers that may get them stuck, they can turn to strategies, tools, or assistance that may be helpful in these situations. When we are faced with a perceived threat, it is a natural response for our brains to get stuck.

This is something to notice and support. When we notice that a student exhibits a change or shift in behavior that seems unusual, it is an opportunity to get curious and start a reflective conversation with metacognitive prompts woven in to increase flexible thinking. In these moments, there may be skills lacking or some other barrier affecting learner performance depending on the situation. Prompting metacognition and reflective thinking can engage learners in the process of noticing what could be getting in their way so that alternative options can be offered. Cultivating strategic approaches to manage challenging situations can increase resilience and propel students into more independent thinking and doing. Ultimately, they will discover their own expertise for how they learn best.

Get Curious! ???

I like to review my work a lot of times, especially on quizzes. It's helpful to check back to be sure I don't miss anything. Whenever I start any assignment, I always check what I have to do, then I like to brainstorm. For my outline, my teachers like to give me the outlining prompts on paper which I don't like. I like outlining on the computer so that I can go back to edit, add, and delete thoughts. When typing, it is easier for me to build off of my original thoughts as I go.

—MIDDLE-SCHOOL STUDENT

As we design learning environments that account for learner variability, it's important to consider questions about how we can support and scaffold efforts for higher-level learning and thinking. We can utilize our own metacognitive skills to support those of our students. Benjamin Bloom and his colleagues (1956) established a framework to categorize educational goals. This framework, known as Bloom's taxonomy, considers different cognitive processes that allow for learners to remember, understand, apply, analyze, evaluate, and create. Years later, Anderson and Krathwohl (2001) revised this framework into *A Taxonomy for Teaching, Learning, and Assessment*, which focuses more on the process of learning rather than just the defined goals (see Figure 7.1). As precursors to the UDL Guidelines, these two taxonomies focus on the interactive nature of learning wherein learners remember, understand, apply, analyze, evaluate, and create.

When supporting metacognitive skills, keep in mind how context and experience can shape and change an individual's perspective.

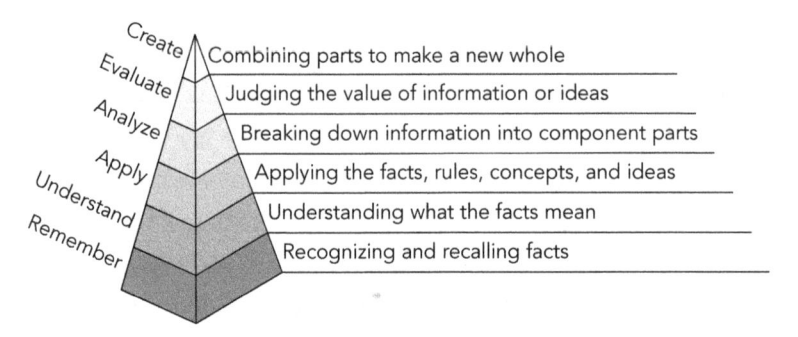

FIGURE 7.1. The revised Bloom's taxonomy

It's also important to consider the different variables that can impact how learners think about a given situation or learning opportunity—including how much they inherently value the task, its relevance to their life circumstances, the resources at their disposal, their available energy and attentional bandwidth, as well as environmental factors that can quickly shift their awareness and focus from the intended task.

Explicit teaching of the metacognition cycle (assessing, evaluating, planning, applying, and reflecting in different situations; see Figure 7.2)—combined with teacher and student modeling of how and why these skills may be employed—can establish options for learners to determine what may be helpful for them to use. You can encourage this by conferencing formally or informally, providing meaningful and authentic feedback, providing suggestions for why and how to use different skills, and, most importantly, embedding resources in the learning environment for all learners to access when needed.

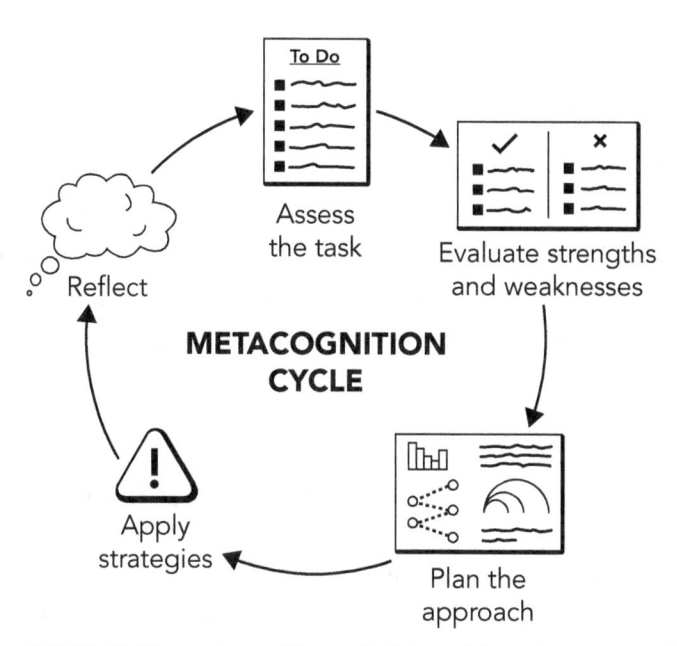

FIGURE 7.2. The metacognition cycle (adapted from Spencer, 2018)

What Helps:

- **Be explicit about the how and the why.** Discussing the context around a topic, activity, lesson, or challenge can transform a student's experience. This helps activate interest and engagement to help them understand why they're working on or toward a specific goal.

    » A common point of challenge for learners who struggle with executive functioning is that if they don't see the purpose or point of a task or lesson, they become further disengaged from the process. Using the UDL Guidelines as a framework to engage students, we want to be explicit about why it is important and helpful in the grander scheme of things, and how it relates to their personal lives and goals.

    » Guiding students along their path to their goals by providing specific and timely feedback presents opportunities for learners to reflect on what is going well or not in their learning process and to change their approach if needed.

- **Be specific with feedback.** Doing so can transform a "That went well" into a more useful reflective moment. An example of this is a learner reflecting on feedback to notice that breaking down an assignment into smaller parts allowed them to focus on one thing at a time and really show what they know.

Use Guiding Questions and Think-Alouds

Asking guiding questions can prompt learners to consider next steps or purposefully guide them to another option or approach.

This technique not only assists students in finding answers but also serves as the foundation for a more robust inner monologue as students start to internalize the sample questions posed and work with greater independence.

Guided questions are most notably connected to reading comprehension, but they can also be used to scaffold executive functioning skills.

Examples of questions to elicit thinking aloud or scaffold strategic thinking include:

- What is my goal and what am I working toward?
- What do I need and how will I reach my goal?
- How can I explain what it is that I don't understand?
- What is the question or uncertainty that is preventing me from moving forward?
- Will I need to break my goal down into smaller parts?
- How will I know when I've reached my goal?

Figure 7.3 shows some prompts for teachers to start meaningful discussions with students.

Verbalizing approaches to thinking helps learners better understand the process of working through a problem or challenge. While faced with a challenge, uncertain scenario, or mistake, educators should share their own self-talk as an opportunity to model for students options to problem-solve, work toward a goal, and reframe a challenge into a point of learning and exploration. In these moments, it is important to prompt reflection about mistakes or pathways that led to stuck points in a constructive and positive way. Showing examples and options for working through a stuck point increases persistence motivation as learners think more flexibly and see alternate paths to reaching their goals.

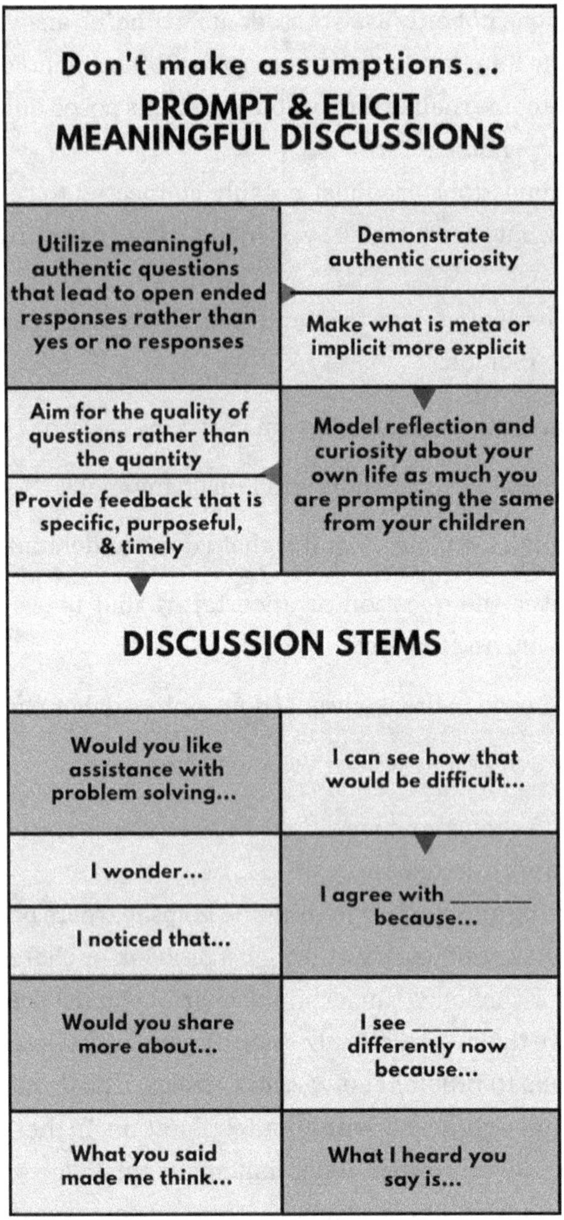

Don't make assumptions...
PROMPT & ELICIT MEANINGFUL DISCUSSIONS

- Utilize meaningful, authentic questions that lead to open ended responses rather than yes or no responses
- Demonstrate authentic curiosity
- Make what is meta or implicit more explicit
- Aim for the quality of questions rather than the quantity
- Model reflection and curiosity about your own life as much you are prompting the same from your children
- Provide feedback that is specific, purposeful, & timely

DISCUSSION STEMS

- Would you like assistance with problem solving...
- I can see how that would be difficult...
- I wonder...
- I noticed that...
- I agree with _____ because...
- Would you share more about...
- I see _____ differently now because...
- What you said made me think...
- What I heard you say is...

FIGURE 7.3. Prompts for meaningful discussions with learners

When teachers model how to think through challenges, uncertain circumstances, or errors, they share their own vulnerability, and as a result learners' willingness to ask questions and adjust their approach to working toward a goal often will increase. Modeling in this way can encourage learners to do the same and present opportunities for teachers to coach them through thinking aloud when they get stuck.

When up against a challenge, show students how to take a step back and map the possible pathways or approaches to solve or get through the challenge (see Figure 7.4).

Provide Timely, Positive Feedback

When learners receive feedback that is specific, supportive, and timely, they are better positioned to more accurately and usefully monitor their progress and stay aware of where they are in the process of learning or completing a task. This process can facilitate and strengthen cognitive flexibility. Rather than saying "Good job" or "That needs some work," giving feedback supported by specific and concrete data about what worked or what could use improvement can transform a learner's ability to think and learn strategically.

Take feedback for writing as an example. Learners often receive marked-up pages that require additional editing. This can help improve a specific piece and is intended to support, guide, and smooth the process of writing. Rather than sharing what can be improved, however, we want to shift our approach to activating points of reflection. Try to focus on conveying *why* learners need to make suggested improvements, not simply pointing out that changes can be made—especially when supporting the writing process and showing learners how to effectively compose ideas in an organized, authentic, and articulate way. There can always be changes or improvements!

Some examples of questions we can ask ourselves before providing specific feedback include:

- How will this teach about what needs to be improved in the future?
- Was there a point of confusion? If so, where did they get confused?
- Is there a barrier that can be shifted to create greater access?
- Are there skills that need to be developed in order to improve their approach? If so, which can be taught, supported, or strengthened?

When providing feedback, think about student strengths to showcase what they're doing well. This is often helpful for learners to hear and acknowledge. Too often, they get stuck on what can be improved, so we want to balance the different points of feedback we offer. Also, when sharing areas to be further developed, consider specific, tangible suggestions first, then explain how those smaller enhancements can improve the larger process or piece they are working on.

Leverage Peer Feedback and Independent Reflection

When the goal and expectations are clear, prepare a rubric or other tool so learners can practice providing peer or self-feedback. These tools can become a part of the process to increase progress monitoring as learners work toward their goals.

Once you've modeled, taught, and practiced with students the process of providing feedback, these experiences can activate multiple means of engagement to practice collaboration: providing each other feedback as well as accepting and utilizing that feedback.

Using scripts and prompts for providing feedback can help scaffold a learner's approach to giving and receiving feedback.

Here are a few examples for giving feedback:

- "I like how you used _____ to illustrate your point."

- "This example really showcased the creative side of your message and demonstrated your understanding of the story by_____."

- "Your careful approach to_____ really showed that you were thoughtful about_____."

- "When you_____ it showed that you_____."

- "What else do you think could have been added here to strengthen your argument?"

- "When you say_____ I think I know what you are trying to communicate, but a reader may be missing_____."

- "What if we thought about this a little differently? Is there another angle or perspective that should also be considered?"

Share your own ideas and examples with us and other readers on X with the hashtag #EFUDL.

Hold Conferences to Facilitate Self-Reflection

A primary function of flexible thinking is the ability to self-monitor and switch directions as needed when approaching a situation. You can help students self-reflect as they move from one completed activity to the next by prompting them to focus on how the learning went. Conferencing to check in with students in a 1:1 or in small group can help them determine which skills and approaches were and were not helpful to accomplish a goal. The focus on reflection can be on how to build stronger, more strategic skills for learning. (If conferencing time isn't available, utilizing student- or teacher-created self-reflection surveys or peer-to-peer conference times incorporated into the process of completing an assignment or project can also emphasize the importance of pausing to self-reflect.)

What Helps:

- When conferencing, **set an agenda** with the student, co-creating and offering a time to listen and facilitate learning.

- **Allow the student to guide the process** and then collaborate to set an agenda together whenever possible. Determine what should be discussed based on a system of priorities.

- **Establish time frames** for each part of the conference and set a timer to guide the process (allowing for flexibility if some extra time is needed, within reason).

- **Set specific checkpoints and a plan** to include action items and next steps.

- When needed, **allow extra time** for reflection, collaboration, or check-ins with a teammate for support.

- **Be present and curious** about why students make certain decisions or take a specific approach in order to glean more information about their perspective.

- **Encourage and model how to provide and accept feedback.** Work together to determine what they need or find most helpful to prepare them to go back to their independent or group work.

- **Offer explicit support** by asking, "How can I best support you to work toward your goals?" to encourage advocacy, iteration, and assistance that builds a classroom culture of shared responsibility for learning.

- **Model and teach skills related to running a conference** and providing explicit, helpful feedback. This includes being specific, timely, and supportive.

- **Have students run a conference or meeting** that incorporates providing feedback, accepting feedback, establishing a plan for next steps, and other points where information needs to be organized and used in some way. These are life skills that will be beneficial to learn early and practice frequently.

Offer Positive Feedback

In the classroom, students are required to follow directions, inhibit impulses, maintain and then shift their attention from one point of focus to the next, and pause before sharing a response to a question, just to name a few. As clinical psychologist Dr. Gerald Reid says on the *ReidConnect-ED* podcast, "Executive function skills are mostly noticed when they are not being used well, and rather than praising behaviors we want to strengthen, adults usually point out when things do not go well or times when they are not being used." By recognizing that this set of skills takes time to fully develop, we can choose to support rather than punish behaviors related to weaker skill use. When students are receiving only negative feedback on what is not going well, they may become shameful and not even recognize what they can be doing differently or what they may doing well already. As educators we can interrupt those systems of stuck or negative thinking by delivering feedback in a way that is timely, specific, and helpful. Rather than thinking in terms of all-or-nothing, positive or negative feedback, we can use language that encourages reflective, critical, and strategic thinking, and focus on the possibilities. The process of learning is not straightforward, so it's likely that learners are exhibiting at least some executive functioning skills.

We must pay attention and notice when this is happening so we can give accurate and timely feedback (as mentioned earlier) to praise behaviors that we want to strengthen or see more of.

Keep Track of Stuck Points

Personal journaling as a point of practice for both writing and reflection is a great activity to build into each week. Whether it's after an assessment, lesson, project, or week, students should pause to assess how it went and jot down some data to keep track of the barriers that may be getting in their way. With this data recorded, learners begin to think more deeply about their approach. Did it work? Should they revisit it to consider a different way forward? What could be tweaked, changed, or kept? This can become a record to review during a conference; a reflection of how a week, project, unit, or segment of time went; and a journal to map out plans or strategies and approaches that are helpful. When we record what is helpful or not, it provides room and space to consider what is possible. When we provide multiple means of representation and perception, students can use audio, video, or text to record their thoughts in the modality that feels most accessible. Ultimately, this could become a guidebook to refer to across space and time.

KEY TAKEAWAYS FROM CHAPTER 7

	CHAPTER SUMMARY	YOUR NOTES
Why should we proactively support executive functioning in learning environments?	Rather than just learning information and completing tasks, we aim for learners to construct new knowledge that they can integrate into their learning, lives, and the greater community they navigate within. Promoting the development of metacognition and reflection establishes opportunities for learners to think about their own thinking, as well as what helps and what doesn't, and determine how they learn best.	
What are the best approaches to supporting learners' executive functioning?	Especially with young learners developing their executive functions, it's necessary to model metacognitive and reflective thinking. Providing prompts, opportunities for practice, and feedback to refine their thinking can strengthen these skills.	
How do I get started?	Begin the practice of reflection, journaling, and verbally sharing ideas about approaches to strategic learning early. When learners are immersed in this practice early on, they can learn from trying out approaches to determine what works best. Hearing other people's reasoning about how learning and work gets done enhances metacognitive skills that become internalized over time. Use and practice guiding questions, prompts, and points of reflection across contexts, content areas, and time to prompt points of deeper thinking and learning.	

8

MINDFULLY DESIGNING A LEARNING ENVIRONMENT TO SUPPORT EXECUTIVE FUNCTIONING

There are ways in which the learning environment can become another teacher. The book *The Third Teacher* (OWP/P Cannon Design et al., 2010) explores the environment as the primary focus in designing opportunities for learning. The authors discuss how intentional design, sensory experiences, and embedded supports provide opportunities for the environment to guide the learning process. When learners know where things are and when events, lessons, or transitions are happening; feel safe and comfortable in their surroundings; and know how to obtain the resources they need, they become empowered to navigate the environment independently with access to supports as needed.

By considering the environment as a third teacher (OWP/P Cannon Design et al., 2010), we can proactively plan through a UDL lens to provide options for executive functioning supports that are accessible to all whenever they are needed.

When planning executive functioning supports for learning environments, we are aiming to increase strategic thinking and learning. Be mindful of what is developmentally appropriate based on the core executive functions: inhibitory control, working memory, and flexible thinking (see also Chapter 3). Then you can consider potential barriers or vulnerabilities where learners would benefit from additional supports or extensions. The goal is to guide learners to determine which executive functioning supports or skills they need in different situations. As discussed previously, building a repertoire of strategies, tools, and approaches can help strengthen strategic learning. Consider executive functioning skills similar to how you might present new content:

- Introduce new strategies or useful tools.

- Model how to use strategies or tools and integrate them into the learning environment, verbalizing when and how you benefit from their use.

- Allow for time and space to practice with support, with feedback, and later independently.

- Provide points of reflection with prompts to identify which strategies or tools are most helpful in different situations.

Establishing the Classroom Climate

Establishing a set of common ground rules or expectations for a learning environment enables all learners, including those who are solidifying their executive functioning skills, to better maintain their goals. When learners understand why expectations or boundaries are in place, it can reduce *cognitive dissonance,* or the conflict that arises when beliefs and behaviors do not align. If students do not feel seen, understood, or heard, they may not be as willing to engage in learning environments without being overly inhibited. When considering multiple means of engagement, we want to cultivate a community that feels connected and respected. This starts with the expectations that the adults in the environment establish. Though we want to build skills for learners to inhibit their impulses, we don't want them to be inhibited to a point where they're not willing to share, contribute, be creative, make mistakes, or explore.

Rather than simply announce or dictate rules of behavior, it's helpful to explain the *why* of those rules. Students across the life span are often more amenable to specific rules when they understand the purpose of the rules and feel the rules are in line with their values. You'll need to establish some non-negotiables for each learning environment or experience, of course, but the idea is that students understand why these are important to the learning community; that they have a shared sense of creating the rules; and that they, too, are working to establish and reinforce those rules to increase comfort, safety, and strategic learning. State the non-negotiables clearly and why they are important, then work together to build ideas and expectations for how to work toward or maintain those expectations together. The co-creation of classroom expectations can set the foundation for how each day goes and the comfort level of everyone in the learning environment. How learners engage—that is, how they show up to all that they do—can become more apparent when there is a framework to work from.

Dr. Phillip Schlechty's (2011) model of levels of engagement during learning is one example of such a framework (see Figure 8.1). In our work with learners, we help them appreciate that there may be times when they're more engaged in their learning or less so.

Attention + Commitment = Level of Engagement

High Attention	High Commitment	**Engagement:** The student associates the task with a result or product that has meaning and value for them. The student will persist in the face of difficulty and will learn at high and profound levels.
High Attention	Low Commitment	**Strategic Compliance:** The task has little inherent or direct value to the student, but the student associates it with outcomes or results that do have value to them (such as grades). The student will abandon work if extrinsic goals are not realized and will not retain what is learned.
Low Attention	Low Commitment	**Ritual Compliance:** The student is willing to expend whatever effort is needed to avoid negative consequences. The emphasis is on meeting the minimum requirements. The student will learn at low and superficial levels.
No Attention	Low Commitment	**Retreatism:** The student is disengaged from the task and does not attempt to comply with its demands, but does not try to disrupt the work or substitute other activities for it. The student does not participate and learns little or nothing from the task.
Diverted Attention	No Commitment	**Rebellion:** The student refuses to do the work, acts in ways to disrupt others, or substitutes tasks and activities to which they are committed. The student develops poor work and sometimes negative attitudes toward formal education and intellectual tasks.

FIGURE 8.1. Schlechty's Levels of Engagement model (adapted from Schlechty, 2011)

This can be true for many different reasons, ranging from interest in a subject, perceived skill, resources to take on the challenge presented, or even how they're feeling at a given moment. When we acknowledge that there is variability in how we show up, even when we care about being engaged, we can help strengthen our awareness of what helps and what might get in the way. It also builds our sense of compassion when someone isn't as fully engaged in one instance as they have been in others. Exploring different situations that may come up, either 1:1 with learners or as a group, helps them recognize that it's okay to be engaged at different levels in different ways at different times. This can normalize the experience of not always being "in the zone" or fully engaged in learning. Sometimes we have a difficult day or face other barriers that interfere with how we show up, and that's okay, especially when we use tools and supports to navigate those moments in time.

Creating Collaborative Working Agreements

When students start thinking of engagement as existing on a spectrum, they begin to develop an awareness and understanding of how to best engage in different learning experiences: what it looks, sounds, and feels like to be engaged, and how they can aim to activate executive functioning skills to participate differently when needed. Utilizing supports to activate executive functioning in these moments can bolster learners' sense of agency and confidence in how they traverse their path. When teachers cultivate a "culture of awareness" around how and when students feel distracted or less engaged, students learn to recognize when they individually experience a shift in focus. Educators can reflect on and discuss, together with the class, what might be interfering with the flow of the class or lesson. This provides an opportunity to introduce and practice options and strategies to reengage—together. Ultimately, pausing to reflect on a distracted or disengaged moment can promote learner agency, where students gain a sense of control over their own learning. These discussions inform the creation of our working agreements, which are based on what everyone in the learning environment wants to get from their time learning together and how they can work collaboratively to achieve those goals.

Students can work together to create this set of agreements in line with what they believe will foster a supportive learning environment. Rather than creating rules, the community determines how they want their learning environment to be and what they want it to feel like. From there, they can work together to operationalize how they will create that environment, how each member can contribute to it, and why it is important to establish these agreements. At different points in time, these agreements can be revisited and adjusted as appropriate to be sure they still reflect the needs of the group. This reinforces the fluid nature of learning—it is not a fixed state but an iterative process that can evolve as needed.

> **Class Agreements**
>
> In order to make the most of our work together, it is important to . . .
>
> - **Respect the process.** All great things take time, patience, and practice.
>
>   We are all here to better understand ourselves, support one another, and learn to best advocate for what helps us most across situations.
>
> - **You are in control of your own learning.**
>
>   We are here to help support, encourage, and guide you . . . and we are in this together.
>
> - **Completing IPW** (independent practice work) is vital to making changes/improvements.

The goal is to allow members of a learning community to work together to emphasize the what, how, and why of the factors that set us up for success. Oftentimes, we do a great job of establishing agreements or expectations together as a class or a group; the agreements serve their purpose; and then, as the year goes on, the helpful behaviors fall away. As mentioned earlier, we do not want to punish behaviors that emerge as skills are still developing.

When it seems like things may have gotten off track, we want to zoom out ourselves to assess what may be needed and what is possible. It is important to check in with learners to determine if the original expectations of the learning environment still match the goals of the classroom or if they need to change. This also models that sometimes our own individual needs change, and therefore our plans or supports need to as well.

What Helps:

- **Start a discussion** using findings from research, a visualization, story, or anecdote to stimulate conversations about behavioral expectations, cultivating engagement, and connecting members as a part of a learning community. The goal is to determine how learners want to feel when they are in a learning environment. The Yale Center for Emotional Intelligence uses a classroom charter in its RULER program to allow students to share how they want to feel while in school and what it will take to get there (*https://www.rulerapproach.org/*).

- **Incorporate Schlechty's model of engagement** to help students self-reflect about how they show up for different types of learning. Discuss what different levels of engagement look like for them and what types of support might help them engage more consistently.

- **Validate** that there may be days when learners are not feeling or performing at their best. What can be done in those situations may be incredibly powerful for learners to hear and talk about together.

- **Establish predictable expectations** to clarify what learners are expected to do and examples of how they can meet those expectations. Doing so may reduce worries connected to uncertainty or perceived lack of skills.

- **Set up a template for learners** to create their own rubric to monitor how they are showing up for lessons each day (see Table 8.1). What are they aiming for, and how might their engagement look different from day to day? This is a helpful tool for students to monitor their own progress and for self-assessment.

TABLE 8.1. A Sample Student Engagement Self-Assessment Rubric

HOW DO WE SHOW UP?	Fully engaged and committed	Present and respectful	Not committed
Attention			
Commitment			
Contribution			
Curiosity			
Practice			
Support			

Minimizing Distractions

As educators we can't always control all the variables in the learning environment. However, we can manipulate the aesthetic, organization, and elements in a space. Considering how a space feels when we enter and work within it can reduce threats and distractions. When we provide multiple means of engagement, we target the reduction of stress on the limbic system and provide additional opportunities to enhance higher-level skills. Sometimes minimal changes can allow for increased cognitive capacity for learning.

When students become more aware of their surroundings, internal tendencies, and how they interact with both, they heighten their awareness of what they can control. When they know what to expect in different situations, they have more options to adjust their approach or environment. Before sitting down for a lesson or work time, they might consider the obvious question, "What do I need?" However, they may not as often ask themselves, "What *don't* I need with or around me?" Noticing the excess "stuff," or tools that could distract them from the task at hand, is the first step to finding options to limit such distractions.

Guiding learners to clear their space, have what they need, and minimize distractions can build the bridge to increase their ability to organize information, set up a plan, and prioritize what needs to get done and how. When learners have some order to their space, they report being better able to access what they need to get started. The fewer points of distraction and less potential for procrastination, the better. This is not to say that every space needs to be pristine and perfectly organized for learning to happen, executive functioning skills to be activated, and work to get done. We can all think of a brilliant professor, teacher, or adult in our lives who always had a remarkably messy desk or pile of things around them.

Distraction is inevitable, and what individuals find distracting is variable. Though attention and executive functioning are not the same thing, they do influence each other. We can be distracted by internal stimuli, like hunger or emotions, or external stimuli, such as sounds, light, movement, and excess "noise." Again, how we respond to distraction can depend on individual characteristics and context as well as our ability to inhibit impulses or refrain from shifting our focus to a less important task. Though we can't always predict or control all the variables that may challenge inhibitory control and attention, we can proactively plan for how to minimize distractions as much as possible—for example, controlling the excess "noise" mentioned earlier, such as certain sounds or lighting, too many wall hangings, disorganized spaces, or other manipulatable stimuli in the environment.

Since distractions can be specific to an individual, it is helpful to encourage students to generate a list of potential distractors or barriers that tend to get them off-task and then identify purposeful steps to address them. Oftentimes, cultivating awareness of what impedes strategic learning is an effective way to teach inhibitory control and increase persistence. If one student is affected by some particular stimulus in a learning environment, it's likely that others are also. Working with students to determine what strategies, breaks, or skills may be helpful increases awareness and motivation and helps to maximize focus and executive functioning activation.

Managing Technology

We know that learning environments designed through a UDL approach acknowledge learners' variable needs and make different types of technology available to help students navigate their learning and day. However, expectations for the use of technology aren't always clear. Similar to establishing routines and expectations for student work, teachers and students need to be abundantly clear about what is responsible use of technology. This may require explicit teaching to fortify responsible and reasonable technology use. Technology of all kinds is a powerful tool, and digital technology can serve as a support, scaffold, or distraction, depending on how it is accessed and used. Minimizing technological distractions is a topic that deserves a full book, so here we'll focus primarily on technology as a tool.

We can teach learners how to use technology such as Chromebooks, iPads, cell phones, smartwatches, and other technological tools to access learning and support executive functioning. Just like other tools, technology needs to be used with intention and purpose. It is important to limit the ways in which technology can distract learners, thereby reducing the need for inhibitory control or at least bolstering motivation to utilize it appropriately.

This is also an important point for educators and adults to model best practices when using their own technology. Learners observe and notice how we interact with different tools. If we exhibit negative interactions, language, frustration, or abuse with technology, those examples send a powerful message to observers. Be mindful to model persistence, and resist giving up on technology if it doesn't work as you intended or expected. Educators can also model their own problem-solving strategies by staying flexible in moments when something doesn't go as planned. Even when we think students aren't paying attention, they are!

Teachers can help students identify and appreciate the ways in which technology is a tool for learning and supporting executive functioning skills by discussing the goal and purpose of different technologies. This is particularly important since technology can often seem geared toward entertainment (e.g., games, shows, social connections) rather than learning. Educators can ask learners to reflect on ways that technology can help them achieve learning goals, as well as ways in which it can distract them from their learning goals. Teachers can also help learners differentiate between educational and entertainment technology use. Oftentimes, when learners report that they are using tablets or computers in school, they say that they're watching YouTube or TikTok or playing games. We don't want to restrict those behaviors—as students will find a way to access what they want, when they want—but rather to teach them when it makes sense to take a break and watch something entertaining.

Put another way, we want to teach learners how to use technology responsibly not by just creating limitations, but by helping them understand how and why technology can be helpful or not helpful. A sixth-grade student learning about habit formation asked Alexis, "So if I do something consistently, it strengthens my brain, right? So if I play games online, is that strengthening my brain?" He was right; it does. Those neural connections will get strengthened the more he plays a game online and fills those dopamine receptors. This moment opened up an opportunity to talk about how his video gaming habit is changing his brain. They talked about the positive impacts of gaming as well as how too much screentime or engaging in video games only as a form of entertainment can impact his brain in a not-so-helpful way. Some studies have shown that too much gaming and screentime can impact sleep, mental health, and expectations outside of the digital environment (Hale et al., 2018). Opportunities can be missed to practice in the real world some of the skills getting reinforced in the digital world. After a short video, discussion, and reflection, the student said, "So, I think I want to only play games online for maybe 20 minutes each day. What about educational videos and apps?" This was another great curiosity that led to a discussion about how screens can be impactful no matter what you're doing, but that educational videos, typing practice, and other tools can be helpful to practice in moderation while being mindful of too much screentime.

To be clear, we are *not* opposed to utilizing technology to support executive functioning development (in fact, Lisa wrote her dissertation on executive functioning and technology!). It is important to utilize digital tools that students have access to in their daily lives through smartphones, tablets, and computers. Teaching and encouraging the use of calendaring systems, timers, or executive functioning apps as scaffolds can help increase behaviors related to progress monitoring, planning, organization, and time management. You may find that some learners find such tools necessary to activate and support executive functioning, while others may or may not benefit from them. Technology tools are only as effective as the way they are taught and practiced. If used appropriately, they can serve as ways to train skills or be used as scaffolds leading to more independent skill use.

Fidgets are a tool that we liken to technology use. In learning environments, fidgets can be a powerful way to increase focus and minimize internal physiological or sensorial distractions. As with technology, when introducing fidgets to learners it is important for them to determine how to use it as a tool to help improve their focus, rather than as a toy that can become distracting to themselves or others. Teaching the benefits of using fidgets, creating points of reflection on how and why they help, and practicing their appropriate use can minimize efforts to manage impulsive behaviors later. One quick and catchy phrase to prompt this reflection is to ask if fidgets or technology are being used as "a tool or a toy?" Eventually, this can become an internalized phrase and narrative to help learners monitor their own distractions while continuing to reflect upon and discuss the purpose and use of each tool.

What Helps:

- **Prompt students to pause and observe** what is happening within or around them is the best first cue for them to consider what is and isn't needed. To develop skills for minimizing distractions, learners must first recognize what the distractions are in their learning environments and interactions. Provide time to pause and ask students what they may or may not need around them during a lesson or independent work time.

- **Initiate a moment of reflection.**

- **Spend time having students create their own checklist** of what is helpful to have with them for lessons (recognizing that context may shift the needs) and work time.

- **Provide time at the beginning, end, or middle of the day** when possible for students to organize their space and gather materials needed for the day or homework.

Whenever possible, consider the needs of learners from a sensorial perspective and adjust as appropriate. It's usually possible to accommodate for physical enhancements in the environment by considering:

- Is the lighting too bright/dark?

- Are there overwhelming smells?

- Is there too much visual stimuli in the environment?

- What's possible to change or adjust?

Teach students to recognize when a tool is meant to relieve stress, increase focus, support skills, or provide movement during work time and how it is helpful. Evaluating which tools are helpful or not is a worthy exercise. Table 8.2 lists some questions that can help add clarifying details to the assessment.

TABLE 8.2. Strategy and Tool Evaluation

WHAT CAN BE USED?	WHY IS IT HELPFUL?	HOW AND WHEN CAN IT BE USED?	OTHER NOTES

When introducing tools to support skills, be explicit about how it is benefiting them. Guide students in a discussion about how and why they may use a digital tool to support their process as they work toward their goals.

KEY TAKEAWAYS FROM CHAPTER 8

	CHAPTER SUMMARY	YOUR NOTES
Why should we proactively support executive functioning in learning environments?	When we emphasize and provide opportunities for learners to take responsibility for their own learning, they gain an awareness about what is most helpful for them and how they can use strategies and skills across contexts. This further strengthens executive functioning development, as learners are trying different ways to approach challenges and learning.	
What are the best approaches to supporting learners' executive functioning?	Have learners determine the resources, energy, and skills they need to employ across different contexts and assignments.	
How do I get started?	Start with multiple means of engagement to have students work together to establish classroom norms and what is expected for learning to happen in the classroom. Encourage discussion and collaboration to determine what is helpful and not helpful to set up strategic learning environments.	

9

SCAFFOLDING LEARNING WITH AGENDAS, TRANSITIONS, ROUTINES, AND BREAKS

Having some knowledge of what's coming next in a given day can help students by minimizing threats and distractions while increasing predictability. When students know how to start, transition through, and end their day, it frees up space for them to be more present, creative, and flexible. With practice, students learn to navigate independently through different parts of their day.

Having predictable routines can minimize stress or worry about how the day will unfold. Though we want to increase flexibility, we also want to support their ability to be flexible. When there is predictability in the day, we can model and support what happens when things change (see the if ... then strategy under "What Helps" in the "Take a Break" section later in this chapter). We can practice routines that help students get started. They can have checklists to provide structure to the way they start their day; help them set up their materials and resources before lessons, activities, or projects; and smooth the transition to the next segment of their day. End-of-day routines ensure they have their assignments and expectations clearly recorded to reference from home as needed and also establish a sense of order and structure, while empowering students to use what is helpful to transition between situations throughout their day. The goal is to increase learners' trust and security in supports established in the learning environment and ultimately in themselves. The more learners can trust that there is some order, predictability, and choice to help them navigate changes in a logical way, the better we're establishing a comfortable environment that promotes emotional regulation and flexibility within that structure.

Keep in mind that spending a significant amount of time and effort practicing routines and modeling examples of how to get started, transition, and clean up learning environments at the beginning of the school year doesn't necessarily mean you won't need to revisit those expectations. At different points of the school year, work with students to determine how to set up their learning environment. Be mindful that even though you've initiated, described, and reviewed routines several times at the start of the school year (or within a specific context, such as for a field trip, special event, lesson, or recess), it's unlikely that all learners will be able to utilize appropriate behaviors and integrate rules or expectations independently. Scaffolds and supports may be necessary for some and serve as a reminder for all. This is especially important when there are changes to the schedule or days off, such as before and after an extended break from school. Helpful reminders and practice (regardless of the age group or developmental level) will reestablish expectations, remind learners of their role and responsibilities in the environment, and reduce additional stressors that may come from not knowing, forgetting, or simply being out of practice.

When we create more predictable situations, learners have a sense of what is to come. This can minimize their stress and uncertainty about how their day will go. For many students, this predictability helps balance their emotions, as they have a point to refer back to when they start to feel uncertain. When they do so, they can be more open to finding clarity in their thinking because they have more resources available to do their work and learning.

Since life and plans have a tendency to change, be sure to prepare learners for changes and establish a solid, predictable foundation for them to work from.

What Helps:

- **Have students create a checklist** of what they can do to prepare for the start of the day, of options for when they finish independent work or during a transition, and of what needs to get completed at the end of the day.

- **Nurture and adapt routines regularly** over the course of the school year, with periodic modeling, practice, and specific praise for the execution of effective routines. Learner and educator needs may shift or change over time. Observing and discussing behaviors that occur prompts reflection about what works and doesn't (and is or isn't helpful) and increases flexibility to collaboratively address what is needed and make appropriate changes as necessary.

Set an Agenda or Schedule

Explicitly stating and posting a schedule of lessons or agenda for a segment of time; content that will be covered in a unit or on an assessment; and activities, events, or the like can help reduce ambiguity that may arise throughout a day. Doing so can neutralize uncertainty and aid in the flow of learning and transitions. Maintaining clarity in expectations and timing for an activity or event can reduce a learner's need for inhibiting distractions or managing the internal distress that emerges from confusion and misunderstandings. As one parent told us, "When the schedule changes, my son has a hard time adapting to that change. When he has a sense of what his role and responsibilities are, he is much better at showing up for school, a new situation, or even a fun activity he is excited about. When I communicate plans clearly, he does better."

Take the time to consider the physical space for the schedule and agenda you set each day. The key is to keep schedules clear and accessible without too much excess "noise" (pictures, colors, designs, etc.) around them. The aesthetic and clarity is just as important as being transparent about how the day is set to unfold. Whenever possible, share expected events and help manage the anticipation or stress around potential changes to allow learners to expend their resources and energy on learning rather than uncertainty or worry.

What Helps:

- **Build in time every morning to preview the day's schedule** before getting started as well as at the end to preview what's coming up in the next day or lesson.

- **Check in** with your physical environment and systems:
  - » Are distractions minimized around the schedule or agenda and is it clear?
  - » Is each event on the agenda simply and clearly stated?
  - » Are there times posted and options for accessing the materials and resources needed for each lesson or activity?

» Are students able to access the schedule when they are outside of your physical learning environment and space?

» Do students have a way to make the schedule their own? Sometimes they may have a different system that works better for them to keep track of what is happening and what needs to get done.

- **Update the schedule and calendar** frequently and consistently—aim for predictability.

- **Digitize and share the schedule** with learners to access and preview.

Monitor Time

Monitoring time is often one of the most challenging tasks for learners of any age, as it's an abstract concept that feels difficult to measure, especially for those with attentional or executive functioning challenges.

Using timers, articulating timing, and providing reminders of remaining time in a lesson, activity, or work period can help learners manage their efforts and allow for time to wrap up in a more strategic way. Rather than abruptly stopping a task or guessing how much time there is left, which can be distracting and unsettling, students can learn to monitor their time or pause their work to shift their attention to the next task in a more mindful and purposeful way.

What Helps:

- **Use both visual and auditory options** to assist with monitoring time. Digital or sand timers can help with visualizing the passage of time.

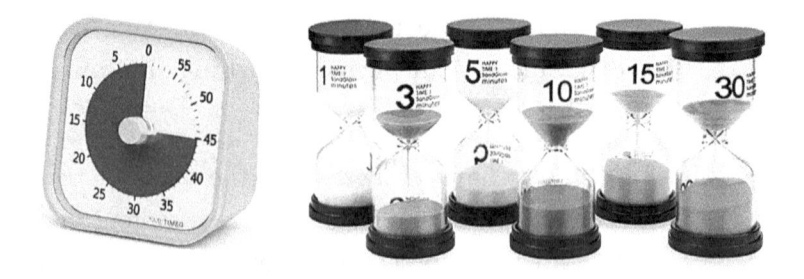

- **Use a tone, chime, or alarm to establish checkpoints** such as 10 minutes, 5 minutes, and 2 minutes until a transition. Haptic tools and wearables that monitor and provide biofeedback can also help if set to vibrate and provide a sensory input to help with managing time.

- **Provide or co-create checklists and reminders** for expectations during transitions. Students can keep checklists (laminated stickers, sticky notes, or any other creative tools) in their space to prompt a transition.

- **Have an agenda for the day or class explicitly posted** and accessible to all. Within a specific activity, it is helpful to set an agenda for the component parts of the lesson, assignment, or situation.

- **Use cues and information to help learners prepare** for what they'll be doing and minimize uncertainty or behaviors that can arise. Doing so also sets the tone for learners to prepare the resources needed and adjust their attention and engagement. Rather than saying it's time for our "Literature Group Lesson" is there a way to cue students to know what they need and what the goal of the lesson will be? Adding visuals or additional notes to the schedule may also help with these types of prompts.

Manage and Support Transitions

Typically, before the end of a semester or right before a school break, students become more lax in the way in which they navigate their environment. There may be environmental changes such as leaving their things around, forgetting homework at home, or being a bit delayed in their transitions between lessons or activities. Without fail, systems or strategies that were working well earlier in the school year start to shift or unravel. When a break in the schedule is approaching, sometimes there's a collective, palpable sense of exhaustion in the classroom, and it can be helpful to assess what's happening and consider adding environmental scaffolds that may not have been necessary earlier in the term or school year. Building in additional time to organize materials and spaces while practicing coping strategies also helps minimize any nerves or anticipation of changes on the horizon. As one third-grade student remarked, "They [the school] gave me this binder to use and it has the schedule in there, but every day something else changes. I feel like I spend so much time just trying to figure out where I need to be and what I need to bring."

To effectively stop one task and transition to another, teachers can explain and model how to "wrap up" a lesson, activity, or work period. Visuals and checklists can support independence with effective transitioning. This is a powerful technique to use across developmental levels. Remember that scaffolding can provide initial supports to allow for effective practice, and then eventually learners can choose which scaffolds are most helpful to prompt transitions or navigate their work time on their own. This scaffolding can be integrated as young as early childhood and is beneficial through university-level learning. Think about the "clean-up song" from early childhood—that same approach is very effective here and can be adapted to signal that students need to wrap up, clean up, and be prepared for an upcoming transition. A common strategy is to use checklists to help prioritize the steps of completing a task or monitoring the process to reach a goal or learning outcome. Rather than establishing this checklist for learners, have them work on what an appropriate flow of a transition might be and what options are available to support them.

Whenever possible, teachers should facilitate learners' use of working memory capacity by making content meaningful and drawing upon familiar or foundational knowledge and understanding.

Many learning environments have a schedule or agenda established each day. The more we can allow for predictability in learners' schedules, the more we can increase their independence in how they navigate each day.

What Helps:
- **Provide visual or verbal prompts** to help learners think about and reflect on where they are in their process:

    "Where am I with my work?"

"Do I need to mark where I left off or make a note for what to do next?"

"Where do my materials go so I can restart again later?"

"What do I need to remember for next time? What will I do next?"

- **Build in ways to scaffold how students follow and use the schedule** to promote the effective use of the schedule itself:
  » Share digital calendars with students and families so they can anticipate what's coming up each week and month.
  » Preview special events, big projects, assessments, and curricula. This allows students to prepare for what's on the horizon.
  » Teach students how to use a planner to map out due dates and events in their own calendars and reinforce their use.
  » Share early and clearly assignments, checkpoints, and due dates for long-term projects or assessments; work or homework to be completed independently; and any other responsibilities. Post assignments on a digital or physical board that all students can access inside and outside the classroom. This allows students and their caregivers to access and check in with assignments to gain clarity or reassurance on expectations.
  » Teach and practice how students can map out their own checkpoints and timelines for units of study, skills to practice, or long-term projects.
  » Emphasize skills and strategies to encourage prioritizing tasks, balancing out time and commitments, and organizing to plan what needs to get completed and when. (See Chapter 5 for specific strategies and ideas to reinforce these skills.)

Using a schedule as an example: if there's a fire drill, a student has a bloody nose, or something else unpredictable comes up, the schedule needs to change. In these instances, it's helpful to share your rationale for how to adjust other components of the day or plan to work around the unanticipated event without derailing the entire day. This is also an opportunity to practice mindfulness and self-regulatory skills to stay calm, patient, and compassionate with yourself and others as you navigate these changes.

At different parts of the school year, students can exhibit different energies or needs. For example, if a vacation, big project, assessment, or even major weather fluctuation is coming up, students may need additional reminders of the expectations and what's on the horizon. This reminder can serve as a way for everyone to organize around the plan and what needs to get accomplished. This is also a good opportunity to check in with students to validate that changes may affect them, so we may need to be more flexible or use different skills to get through it. When possible, we want to encourage students to use their own judgment and process to prepare for whatever may come up.

This also presents an opportunity to teach coping skills for a change or transition. It's important to be mindful of our delivery and show compassion around having to change and make a new plan. This helps to minimize additional anxiety and maximize learners' ability to inhibit impulses and pause to plan mindfully.

Take a Break

Over the years, our ever-changing world and technology advances have diminished attention spans quite a bit. When looking around in the classroom during a lesson or work time, we may identify learners who need a break to refocus and shift back to their work. It's often difficult for these learners to inhibit emotional or behavioral urges that come up when they need to focus on a specific task, especially if they perceive that task as challenging or inaccessible.

In our fast-paced world, it's important to recognize the value of a break or a pause. As adults, in our own day-to-day lives, we recognize the benefit of taking a break but don't always feel like we have time or permission to indulge and do so. In our own work, both of us build in times for meditation and moments to pause, and also intentionally step away from our work, to strengthen our own wellness. Over the years, we've realized that to avoid falling into the trap of taking on too much, we have to balance the many wonderful opportunities we've been honored to be a part of with regular breaks. When we press pause, we give ourselves some distance from a task or interaction and an opportunity to find quiet and clarity to do our best work for ourselves and others. The airline advice that we need to put on our oxygen mask first and then help others is a reminder that we need to take care of ourselves so that we can show up and do well for others.

For learners, it is important to cultivate a sense of awareness so they, too, will notice when they need a pause or break and recognize that they have options for what to do next. We know that context makes a difference, so what works in one situation might not be appropriate in all situations. As we facilitate the process of teaching awareness to support attention, emotional regulation, and executive functions, we may need to be more purposeful and explicit than usual. It's often helpful to take the skills and strategies we implicitly know are helpful or do naturally as adults and make them more explicit. Evaluating what is and isn't helpful in different situations can solidify a student's understanding of what they can do to get started on a task, proceed mindfully through a lesson or activity, and monitor their own progress as they work toward a goal. Table 9.1 shares some prompts for this evaluation.

TABLE 9.1. A Sample Evaluation of Behaviors That Are and Aren't Helpful

HELPFUL	WHY?	NOT HELPFUL	WHY?
Holding a *pomodoro session*: 25 minutes of uninterrupted work (taking a short break midway). Keep it going!	Doing uninterrupted work for short bursts	Using smartphone too much	Distracting
Gathering materials before the next class	Being prepared	Following fantasy basketball/ football/ sports in general	Overdoing it and learning too much about all the players and teams
Eating more healthily (good breakfast), staying hydrated	Having a more consistent energy and mood improves motivation	Watching YouTube	Being hooked in by their algorithms
Detaching from current task—showering, driving, listening to music	Unhooking and resetting to be able to do the work	Sleeping with the phone nearby	Staying too connected; too easy to use before bed and upon waking up
Exercising during lunch breaks	Getting the day going and feeling more locked in for work	Playing video games	Losing track of time
Drinking water first thing in the morning	Helping wake up in the morning	Being asked by parents or others if the work is done yet	Taking away from the work
Setting an intention for starting the day (making bed, eating breakfast, exercising)	Setting up for a more productive day	Saying, "I'll do this later"	Running out of time, which creates more work and stress
Making a to-do list and breaking up each item into smaller tasks	Minimizing the overwhelm to focus on more attainable subtasks	Subscribing to the "toolbox fallacy": "I can do this, once I have this . . . or once this is in place"	Making excuses and procrastinating. Instead, do an intermediary step to get started—just get started!
Having nicer weather and more sunlight	Not having to prepare for bad weather/early dusk		

HELPFUL	WHY?	NOT HELPFUL	WHY?
Moving headphones from phone to laptop	Focusing on what needs to be done on the computer		
Taking advantage of nature, sunlight, the outdoors	Getting a little vitamin D goes a long way		

Take a moment right now to press pause, stop reading, and take a breath. With those few seconds of intentionally stopping what you are doing, did you notice a difference? Did you lose track of where you were before you paused from reading? Or do you feel refreshed and refocused to continue to the next line?

As you might imagine, being able to press pause when we're feeling dysregulated, overly challenged, or confused can help us think more clearly and increase cognitive flexibility. Being able to press pause gives your learners time to inhibit an urge or behavior and allows them to identify what choice is best or decide what comes next. These are, however, skills that develop over time and need to be practiced.

It is important to teach, practice, and support recognizing when you need a break as well as how to efficiently take one. Being immersed in a flow state can be incredibly beneficial for creativity, working toward and accomplishing goals, and learning new things. However, a realistic goal is one that balances focused work time with nourishing other aspects of ourselves so we don't fall into an all-or-nothing, this-or-that mindset.

As one high school senior shared: "We have talked about what things are most important to me on a personal level which one could be, you know, I love the outdoors. I love going on hikes, that kind of thing. I love playing guitar. I love music, I think it's a balance of prioritizing, you know, grades in school and those sort of like, things you need to do well and to do to get by in the world and also balancing your interests. And I think at the end of the day, you realize that those things also complement each other."

When working with learners, ensure that your work together is not just about academics. As mentioned earlier, it's essential to care for the whole person in order to work toward your goals. This is where self-care, awareness training, and monitoring progress comes in. Offer opportunities for learners to mindfully choose a reasonable option—stretching, getting a drink of water, coloring—for a brief rest or pause from their work. A break doesn't encourage task avoidance but instead recharges the learner's attention and resources before they return to or shift from the task.

What Helps:

- **Options to take a break:**
  - » **While at my desk:** Stretch, doodle, do 12 finger tap affirmations, journal, or take a quick and quiet reflective moment.
  - » **For 1 minute:** Stand up to stretch, shift to another seat in the classroom to increase focus, get a drink of water, engage a visualization exercise, do mindful breathing, or choose another restorative option.
  - » **For 3-5 minutes:** Take a quick walk, get a snack, listen to a song, dance, or do wall push-ups, jumping jacks, or another exercise.

What Helps:

- **Establish if . . . then scenarios** like "*If* you finish step 1, *then* you can take a quick break by [insert a break option they've previously identified that makes sense, meets their goal, and won't get them completely off track]."

- **Build in options and times** to take a break, monitor progress, and increase persistence and motivation (see Table 9.2 for some prompts).

TABLE 9.2. Options for Staying On Track: Suggestions from a High School Student

IF...	I END UP FEELING...	INSTEAD I CAN...	WHY?
I say, "I'm going to do all of these things, I just need to check my homework first" and I don't complete anything	Embarrassed and guilty that I didn't get anything done	• Preview and prioritize the work with Mom to list out what homework needs to get done. • Set timer for 5 minutes. • List homework in planner. • Check email and classrooms with mom for any changes to work.	• Helps to practice making a plan and limits my online time where I could easily get distracted and off track • Will eventually do this on my own • Start to set limits and not get off track • Sets expectations so Mom knows my plan
I have set up my plan for homework	• Like I have too much to do • Good about what I need to do	• Rather than worry about what needs to get done, break it into smaller parts. • Brainstorm and create an outline. • Start with just one paragraph of reading and notes. • Take short (1–3 minute) breaks in between as needed. • Set a timer and get started on at least one thing.	• Helps to preview the work • Helps to check the facts of what the expectations actually are/clarity of the assignment • Empowers me to work independently

(continued)

TABLE 9.2. Options for Staying On Track *(continued)*

IF . . .	I END UP FEELING . . .	INSTEAD I CAN . . .	WHY?
I get distracted doing a task	• Worse or panicked if I miss something • Happy or excited	• Find a way to quickly reset my focus. • Pause and take a few breaths.	• Prevents getting stuck • Helps to reset expectations and be reasonable • Give myself permission to reset—we all get distracted sometimes

- **Assess available resources** to determine how much energy, focus, and time they must dedicate to reach a goal. We have found that individuals have approximately 15–20 minutes of focused time on a task at a time. When considering a lesson, independent work times, or scaffolding to support attention and focus, consider developmental norms for attention and variability in learners' attention.

- **Do the Triple A exercise.** What do we need: A breath? A break? Assistance?

    The Triple A exercise can be a good reference point to consider what may be helpful in that moment. As one fourth-grade student shared: "Whenever I know something is getting too tough or too much, I need to think about what I need in that

Triple A
What's Needed...
A Breath?
A Break?
Assistance?

@AlexisAnnReid

situation. Triple A helps me to figure out what to do. Sometimes I forget to use it, but those are the times when I just stay stuck and usually end up with too much other stuff to do later."

Pause and assess what is needed and proceed mindfully from there.

Additionally, teachers can plan for a break by using a timer to budget out how long a learner estimates something should take to complete, which will help them determine when they should take a break, shift to a different task, or ask for assistance if needed. Table 9.3 offers some guidance for effective scheduling and break time.

TABLE 9.3. How Are You Scheduling and Planning Your Day?

EFFECTIVE SCHEDULES AND PLANS	EFFECTIVE BREAK OPTIONS
• Add reminders in phone calendar. • Ask for accountability. • Write a full list of all tasks and assignments due for the week. Highlight at least two assignments to start with each day. Cross out as you complete each task. Set up a plan each day. • Reach out to teachers if you're having a hard time getting work done, have questions, or will be delayed in turning something in. • Use a planner (online or paper). • Take things one day (sometimes one hour) at a time: aim for short-term plans and be flexible! • Break things down into smaller parts to get started. • JUST GET STARTED!	• Exercise. • Take a movement break. • Dance. • Have a smoothie. • Pet, walk, or play with a pet. • Go for a walk. • Get outside. • Engage in productive procrastination: What can you get done during the in-betweens (email, cleanup, adjust plan, etc.)? • Draw or doodle. • Write, listen to, or play music. • Have a snack.

Limiting time on-task to small chunks can reduce the number of distractions that could emerge when students are working on one task for extended periods of time, thereby preserving inhibitory control resources. Educators should assess how much time on-task makes sense for the learners they are working with.

A survey, a challenge, or 1:1 check-ins with learners can help educators collect data on how much time to offer students taking on different learning tasks. From there, educators can scaffold and build in times to take breaks, embed signposts to prompt pauses for reflection, or establish milestones for learners to pause and then determine what comes next and is needed for their process.

Learners can also be encouraged to assess and monitor their time using tools like sand timers, the Time Timer visual timer, an app, a watch, or a kitchen timer. Understanding how much time is available can help prompt reflection for learners to identify when they need to take a breath, pause for a break, ask for assistance, or shift activities.

A *pomodoro session* is a frequently used technique where for every 25 minutes of focused work time, you schedule and take a 5-minute break. After 4 "pomodoros" (Italian for *tomato*), you take a longer 10- to 15-minute break. The idea is to treat the focused work time as a game to "collect" as many tomatoes/pomodoros as you can.

Another way to help students be mindful of distractions and assert inhibitory control is to proactively plan for when more challenging tasks will be initiated. The times when a greater reserve of attention and energy is available are likely better opportunities for students to take on more challenging tasks. As noted earlier, when we have too much going on or "on our plates" and are feeling worn out, it may be more challenging to activate our executive functioning skills.

Determining when learners have more or less energy throughout the day, as well as recognizing which tasks will be more or less challenging to them, can allow for proactive planning to help you assess what is needed.

Have learners think about what resources they need to be successful. Doing so allows them to dedicate the most focused time on a challenging task versus when they should focus on less demanding tasks. This is when they consider what they need, how they are feeling, and what is possible. Table 9.4 shows an example they can use to guide them in this reflection.

TABLE 9.4. What Gets in the Way and What Is Possible?

TASK	FEELING OR BARRIER	PROBLEM	AVAILABLE STRATEGIES	POSSIBLE SOLUTIONS
Start homework	Math is not my favorite class and I can't usually focus during the 8:30 a.m. class, so I have no idea what to do. I don't want to look like I "don't get it" and am worried asking will annoy the teacher. We were supposed to know what he taught today even before the class met. It is only one problem set to finish; it shouldn't take that long.	I am starving and did not eat yet today. I have no clue how to use the equations to solve the three questions. If I don't do it, I won't lose too many points or bring my score down that much. There are so many other things I could do better right now.	Start with: • Reframing the situation: This is *not* an all-or-nothing situation. • Asking your teacher or a classmate who does well in the class to break down one problem so you have an example to work from. • Checking online to get an example of breaking it down.	• Check in with your teacher to ask for one example or to be sure you are doing it correctly. • Have your friend meet you after school to walk you through the problem. • Finish at least two problems with your friend, checking to ensure it's going well before leaving.

Learners can plan to initiate more challenging tasks when energy is available, since inhibitory control may be weaker when energy levels are low and demands are high. These skills can be scaffolded and modeled through lessons and activities to practice estimating time and managing challenges or different levels of demands.

Make it a game! Challenge students to make time estimates throughout their day of how long it will take to complete different tasks. This can be done inside and outside the classroom.

The goal is not to race but to thoughtfully estimate how much time they think it will take to complete different tasks. Work with learners to generate the list of tasks for their time estimates. Oftentimes learners who have executive functioning challenges struggle with understanding and monitoring the passage of time.

The more they can be directed to the amount of time that passes, actively think about how much time is needed, and start to realize that things may take more or less time than expected, the more comfortable and confident in initiating tasks they will likely feel.

KEY TAKEAWAYS FROM CHAPTER 9

	CHAPTER SUMMARY	YOUR NOTES
Why would setting up approaches to co-create a learning environment that values agency and strategic learning support executive functioning skill development?	The UDL Guidelines provide the framework to map out how providing options for engagement help minimize threats and increase agency in learning environments. Establishing systems from the outset of design promotes collaboration, comfort, and trust in the process to showcase the benefits for executive functioning skills as learners take greater risks and expand their strategic learning. When learners have space and tools to practice strategic learning, they can increase engagement and collaboration.	
What are the steps and stages that make the most sense for you to incorporate into your learning environment?	Establishing a comfortable and safe space allows learners to activate their skills as they practice and solidify what works best for them across different situations. Helping learners practice using different tools and approaches while developing an awareness of what helps will build their confidence and skills for strategic learning.	
How do you think your learners will respond to the adjustments you intend to make as you explicitly share that they are being used to support executive functioning development?	Every educator will think about and choose what works best for them to integrate into their learning environment. Simply considering options to support engagement and executive functioning shows the learners you work with that you value their unique perspectives, experiences, and processes. Start with what you already do and know, then intentionally add in what you think will be possible to integrate and practice consistently.	

10

USING MINDFULNESS, MOVEMENT, AND THE ARTS TO SUPPORT EXECUTIVE FUNCTIONS

As mentioned in earlier chapters, executive functions have a significant relationship with academic, social, and health outcomes for children and adults. Helping learners develop better executive functioning strategies and skills can have a lasting benefit. There are many research studies looking into computer-based training, exercise, music, martial arts, and other practices that might boost executive functioning among learners. For the purposes of this book, we'll focus on the evidence-based (that is, supported by multiple peer-reviewed scientific studies) and promising (meaning there is some supporting peer-reviewed research but not enough to be evidence-based) practices that can support executive functioning development.

Many studies of executive functioning development programs discuss *generalizability*. This refers to the intervention's ability to impact executive functioning within everyday life, not just in the context of the intervention. For example, while some computer training programs show a significant boost in executive functioning related to software use, this increase hasn't been found to transfer to other aspects of the participants' lives. Our goal as educators should be to maximize transfer of skills, so we'll focus only on interventions, practices, and programs that have demonstrated good generalizability in increasing executive functions in everyday life.

> ### ⏱ Notes From the Field
>
> I had the amazing experience of hearing executive functions experts Adele Diamond and Martha Denkla speak about the importance of joy in learning and executive functioning development at a talk in November 2018. These two experts agreed that meaningful activities that push you outside of your comfort zone while *joyfully* engaging you are the most promising avenue for executive functions development. I was nearly jumping out of my seat with excitement. Here were two famous women at the top of their field asking educators to make learning joyful and engaging!
>
> —LISA

Teaching Strategies for Executive Functioning Development

Two different organizations that vet evidence-based instructional practices and interventions, the What Works Clearinghouse and Evidence for ESSA, list *reciprocal teaching*—in which teachers and students take turns in the role of instructor to discuss reading content—as a method that enhances students' flexible thinking. Research indicates that the practice of reciprocal teaching can impact reading comprehension by supporting higher-order cognitive skills. This approach falls under a category of instructional practices known as *cognitive apprenticeship*, a method of instruction incorporating modeling, with scaffolded coaching in the form of guiding questions. Rather than providing the learner with answers, the instructor asks questions to help the learner arrive at the answers themselves.

Models of cognitive apprenticeship allow students to build an internal monologue that assists with identifying a problem, determining multiple options for approaching the problem, initiating a strategy, monitoring whether the strategy is working, and shifting to another potential solution if the first strategy doesn't yield the desired results. In summary, cognitive apprenticeship approaches to instruction help students develop higher-order executive functions by making the internal thought processes of a strategic learner more "visible" than they are for a novice.

What do Tools of the Mind, PATHS, Montessori, and reciprocal teaching all have in common? A specific focus on the instructor as a mentor or coach who avoids giving answers and instead asks guiding questions to help students come to productive conclusions and solutions. Guiding questions and mentoring were also found to explain the gains in working memory participants experienced in studies conducted by Cogmed, a research-based training program designed to improve the brain systems responsible for attention and working memory. It's a pretty safe bet that using guiding questions as an instructional strategy will help students develop stronger executive functions while learning important academic content. We can use elements of the cognitive apprenticeship model (Collins et al., 1991) to leverage best practices in mentorship and coaching to improve not only academic learning but executive functions as well.

Elements of cognitive apprenticeship (adapted from Collins et al., 1991):

- **Modeling:** Demonstrating what the learners will be doing while using "think aloud" strategies to make thinking "visible" to the group.

- **Coaching:** Observing learners in action, providing mastery-oriented feedback, and offering assistance when needed.

- **Scaffolding:** Providing supports for students as needed to complete learning tasks.

- **Articulation:** Encouraging learners to use "think aloud" strategies to highlight their own thinking and provide greater opportunities for coaching.

- **Reflection:** Encouraging learners to reflect on their work as well as the work of their peers.

- **Exploration:** Inviting learners to use the curriculum as a jumping-off point for further questioning, research, and problem-solving.

Mindfulness

The idea of using mindfulness to increase conscious awareness, cognitive skills, and overall health and well-being is not novel. These practices can be found in both modern and ancient religions. Though most often tied to Buddhist teachings and practice, mindfulness and meditative practice are found in most religions. Since the late 1970s, however, mindfulness has become more of a mainstream practice to evoke a sense of center, calm, and awareness rather than only a spiritual or religious experience. Mindfulness-based interventions (MBIs) may include both passive (e.g., breathing techniques, visualization, progressive muscle relaxation, and body scanning) and active activities (e.g., walking, tasting, listening, or integrating hand-eye coordination for games or practice). Depending on the goal, frequency, and quality of the exercise, MBIs have been shown to increase awareness, focus, and concentration. Teaching these skills early, modeling them, and encouraging practice in non-stressful moments can make them an option available to learners in times of need.

A recent review and meta-analysis of MBIs suggest that mindfulness can aid our ability to control our attention, which, in turn, can increase self-regulation (Leyland et al., 2018). This increased attentional control may help a person recover from negative feelings and enact executive functioning skills when needed.

What does this mean in the classroom? Developing students' mindfulness skills would be a worthwhile investment. It helps students recognize when they are becoming distracted, need a break, or need assistance. This acknowledgment or awareness can increase their self-regulatory skills, allowing them to maintain momentum in their work by activating executive functions. In times when learners feel challenged, are overwhelmed, or have negative feelings that can otherwise become a roadblock or disengage their executive functioning, using mindfulness can turn a potential point of frustration into a teachable moment.

From a sixth-grade student: "One of the best ways to find your focus and relax your mind is to practice a mindfulness exercise. People who can't concentrate, calm themselves down, or simply struggle to sleep can all use these exercises. These exercises can be as simple as focusing on your breathing to as complex as visualizing your thoughts floating away. The goal of a mindfulness exercise is to let go of your thoughts so you can make room for whatever you are trying to accomplish. A great thing about these is that you can do an exercise almost anytime and anywhere. [Whether] it be at work, school, or even on a plane, taking a few seconds to do a mindfulness exercise can make a world of difference in your regular activities.

Ultimately, the purpose of mindfulness is to have a healthier and happier everyday life."

Research has shown promising results from school-based mindfulness programs; however, it may be challenging for teachers to build these skills effectively (Zenner et al., 2014). The more mindfulness is practiced, modeled, and encouraged for all, the greater the benefit. Popular programs that teach about how the brain develops and how to exercise or strengthen it through mindfulness include MindUp, Mindful Schools, and the Mindfulness in Schools Project (MiSP).

Options to integrate these approaches into classrooms include the following:

- Include mindful moments as part of the day, either to center and begin a lesson or class or afterward (but before a reflection).

- Pause for reflection when starting, during, or after work, or to determine highlights or points of gratitude for your day. Or play games and provide opportunities to reflect with others in the classroom.

- Provide sensory tools or calming music (putty, stress balls, calming scents or smells, mindfulness jars, etc.).

- Close your eyes and imagine a moment where you felt joy and success in something you did. Envision yourself in that moment.

- Use progressive muscle relaxation: Tense up different parts of the body then release and relax.

- When the focus is on the breath, learners can choose which practice best suits them:

- » Belly breathe: Feel the belly expand and deflate like a balloon as it is filled and emptied of air.

- » Buddy breathe: Gently place a stuffed animal on the abdomen or chest to show the rise and fall that occurs in the body with each deep breath.

- » Deeply inhale and then exhale slowly as if blowing out birthday candles.

- » Imitate the action of slowly and purposefully blowing up a balloon.

- » Slowly blow bubbles to create as many or as big of a bubble as possible.

- Allow for mindful movement and stretching to connect with the body and ground and center oneself.

- Provide images or materials to draw, or color repeated patterns.

- Have learners share how they practice mindfulness. Use this collection of ideas as options for other students to draw from when needed.

Arts and Music

Several studies have found a correlation between studying arts and music and stronger executive functioning skills (Diamond, 2013; Hardiman et al., 2014; Rinne et al., 2011). While it's not clear if there's a cause and effect between the arts and executive functions, it's promising that several studies of arts-integrated instructional approaches showed greater gains than non-arts-based comparison groups in academic testing. This lends support to the correlational studies pointing to a strong relationship between the arts, learning, and executive functioning skills.

Exercise

Research on exercise and executive functioning is very promising (Diamond, 2015). This makes sense: after all, your brain is part of your body. A healthy body supports a healthy brain (Denckla, 2018).

According to an analysis of nearly 20 research studies, acute exercise (e.g., 10–40 minutes) has a positive impact on inhibitory control (an essential element of learning and self-regulation) among preadolescents, adolescents, and young adults (Verbugh et al., 2014). A more recent meta-analysis of studies that used physical activity interventions with children found increases in working memory, inhibition, higher-level executive functioning skills (e.g., planning, problem-solving), and metacognitive skills (Alvarez-Bueno et al., 2017). Additionally, these authors note that physical activities with greater cognitive demands may also improve one's efficiency of inhibitory control. Diamond (2015) suggests that engaging in physical activities that require executive functioning skills might be the most effective.

> The first week I started waking up earlier to exercise before going to school, I immediately noticed a difference. I was able to stay on track with my classes, not get up to use the bathroom every day during the same classes, at the same time, and follow through on the things I knew I had to do. It is almost like I decided to self-discipline myself by setting a schedule for exercise, but somehow, I am not being disciplined at all, my body feels better, confidence is increasing, and I am more clear with what I have to do in and out of classes.
> —HIGH SCHOOL JUNIOR

Though findings suggest that exercise interventions have a positive impact on executive functioning skills, they produce the weakest effects of other interventions studied (Diamond & Ling, 2016, 2019). Though aerobic activities, resistance training, and yoga may exhibit weak effects on executive functioning skills, that does not indicate no effect. Other mind-body activities like taekwondo, t'ai chi, Chinese mind-body practices, and Quadrato motor training also point to positive effects on executive functioning.

What Can Schools and Teachers Do With These Research Findings?

Taken together, these research findings can help educators design flexible learning environments that support learners' executive functioning. Some of these findings will make more sense for you than others, just as some will feel more comfortable to integrate. Ultimately, you want to determine which new approaches are in line with your values, goals, and availability within your learning environment. You can also have learners create their own curriculum, research experience, or activity related to specific content, skills, and goals. This can help initiate the learning process and enable different learners to share their perspectives.

Here are a few key takeaways from the research:

- Establish a flexible physical learning environment.

- Make spaces to stand, roll, wiggle, move around, stretch, or lean while working and listening.

- Allow for nontraditional spaces for collaboration, partner work, or independent quiet work.

- Allow for breaks and practice movement in learning.

- Brainstorm and establish expectations for respectful and helpful breaks.
- Determine what physical movement helps to promote focus, executive functioning activation, and opportunities to recenter on a task.
- Teach seated stretches or yoga.
- Have learners lead movement breaks, games incorporating hand-eye connections, or big stretches before an important part of the day.
- Have each learner build a toolkit of what they can use at different points in time.
- Educate learners about the benefits of exercise and overall wellness on learning and the brain:
  » How does physical activity promote the activation of executive functioning skills?
  » Why is it beneficial?
  » What happens to the brain when we exercise?
- Encourage physical expression for learners responding to discussion questions or showing what they know.
- Games like charades or acting out skits can be creative and physical ways to demonstrate knowledge.

Final Thoughts

If you picked up this book and made it to the end, we're willing to bet that you've worked with students who have struggled with executive functioning. As we said earlier, we've been there too. It can be *frustrating* to see a student struggle and not be able to pinpoint why or what to do about it. We have never met a teacher who didn't want to find a way to make things better for their students. It's what makes teachers *amazing*. Just picking up this book and thinking about how to better provide options for executive functions makes you a UDL rockstar—and an executive functioning advocate.

We set out to write this book because every time we talked to teachers about executive functions, we witnessed their excitement over finally having a name to put to the struggles they observed in classrooms. We know from experience that often educators read the UDL Guideline "Provide options for Executive Functions" and feel a bit lost. But we've also found that once teachers have a deeper understanding of what executive functions are and how they develop during the K–12 years, they can eagerly jump in and start effectively supporting students with great success. Just as we mentioned the benefits for students understanding the "why" and "how," we hope this book has provided more clarity around this goal of the UDL Guidelines and especially around working toward improving executive functioning.

Supporting executive functions isn't fancy work. But it isn't time-consuming drudgery, either. It's intentionally thinking about how much a learning environment might stress students' executive functioning skills and then coming up with ways to lighten the load when needed. The support examples we presented in Part 2 of this book all came from an understanding of executive functions mixed with creative problem-solving. Teachers already possess creative problem-solving skills in abundance, so all we needed to do was explain executive functions and brain development in a way that's relevant to those who teach K–12 students.

We also recognize that as educators, we each have our own set of executive functioning skills that we bring into each day. Perhaps while reading this book, you've recognized some habits or behaviors that you, too, find challenging. Being human is to experience challenges, struggles, and frustrations—but also to be curious, patient, and supported. When we recognize our own skills and strengths, as well as areas to be developed, we can share the greatest human opportunity we have: to be vulnerable. When we are real with ourselves about what we can do, enjoy, and need support with, we can also find empathy for ourselves and those we work with or are around. This empowers us to make improvements while supporting others. Believe us, many of the same strategies we offer here have been instrumental in our lives and journeys personally, professionally, and in the creation of this book. We get it, and hope the discussions and ideas shared here empower you to also support yourself and those in your life. Self-care and self-actualization is not selfish. Sharing vulnerabilities, being authentic, and co-creating with the learners we work with establishes a partnership that will likely transcend your time with them in any learning environment. These are the moments where real learning transforms the confines of space and time.

This book was never intended to be read through once. We envisioned it as a useful reference for when you're planning or feeling stuck. Write in the margins. Take notes; jam it full of stickies! Above all, share with each other! Once you take what you've learned about executive functions and start to "provide options to support executive functions" in your learning environments, take pictures, take notes, write down descriptions, and share! Did you try out a strategy from this book and it didn't work? Let us know and let's problem-solve as a community. This book is only step 1 in providing teachers with the knowledge to amplify the learning experiences of all students. The next steps involve elevating your voices and experiences so that we can all learn together and make even more improvements. Here's how you can share:

- Tweet *@EF_UDLchat* or *@AlexisAnnReid*

- On Instagram, see *@AlexisAnnReid* or *@EquitableAccess*

- Email us at *Alexis@ReidConnect.com* and *Carey@KennedyKrieger.org*.

- Attend UDLIRN/CAST UDL Summit or other CAST UDL conference events and find us.

We hope to see you out there!

References

Álvarez-Bueno, C., Pesce, C., Cavero-Redondo, I., Sánchez-López, M., Martínez-Hortelano, J. A., & Martínez-Vizcaíno, V. (2017). The effect of physical activity interventions on children's cognition and metacognition: a systematic review and meta-analysis. *Journal of the American Academy of Child and Adolescent Psychiatry, 56*(9), 729–738. https://doi.org/10.1016/j.jaac.2017.06.012

Anderson, L. W., & Krathwohl, D. R. (2001). *A taxonomy for learning, teaching and assessing: A revision of Bloom's taxonomy of educational objectives: Complete edition.* Longman.

Baggetta, P., & Alexander, P. A. (2016). Conceptualization and operationalization of executive function. *Mind, Brain, and Education, 10*(1), 10–33. https://doi.org/10.1111/mbe.12100

Baird, A., Fugelsang, J., & Bennett, C. (2005, April). *What were you thinking: An fMRI study of adolescent decision-making.* [Poster presentation]. Twelfth Annual Cognitive Neuroscience Society (CNS) Meeting.

Blair, C. (2016). Developmental science and executive function. *Current Directions in Psychological Science, 25*(1), 3–7. https://doi.org/10.1177/0963721415622634

Blair, C., & Ursache, A. (2011). A bidirectional model of executive functions and self-regulation. In K. D. Vohs & R. F. Baumeister (Eds.), *Handbook of self-regulation: Research, theory, and applications* (pp. 300–320). Guilford Press.

Bloom, B. (1956). *Taxonomy of educational objectives, Handbook: The cognitive domain.* David McKay Company.

Carey, L., & Jacobson, L. (2017, June 13). *Faculty interview with Dr. Lisa Jacobson: What should teachers know about childhood cancer survivors?* Linking Research to Classrooms. https://www.kennedykrieger.org/stories/linking-research-classrooms-blog/faculty-interview-dr-lisa-jacobson-what-should-teachers-know-about-childhood-cancer-survivors

Carey, L. B., Schmidt, J., Dommestrup, A. K., Pritchard, A. E., van Stone, M., Grasmick, N., Mahone, E. M., Denckla, M. B., & Jacobson, L. A. (2020). Beyond learning about the brain: A situated approach to training teachers in mind, brain, and education. *Mind, Brain, and Education, 14*(3), 200–208. *https://doi.org/10.1111/mbe.12238*

Collins, A., Brown, J. S., & Holum, A. (1991). Cognitive apprenticeship: Making thinking visible. *American Educator, 15*(3), 6–11.

Covey, S. R. (1989). *The seven habits of highly effective people: Restoring the character ethic.* Simon and Schuster.

Denckla, M. B. (2018). *Understanding learning and related disabilities: Inconvenient brains: Meanings, functions, and ambiguity.* Routledge.

Diamond, A. (2013). Executive functions. *Annual Review of Psychology, 64,* 135. *https://doi.org/10.1146/annurev-psych-113011-143750*

Diamond, A. (2015). Effects of physical exercise on executive functions: Going beyond simply moving to moving with thought. *Annals of Sports Medicine and Research, 2*(1), 1011.

Diamond, A., & Ling, D. S. (2016). Conclusions about interventions, programs, and approaches for improving executive functions that appear justified and those that, despite much hype, do not. *Developmental Cognitive Neuroscience, 18,* 34–48. *https://doi.org/10.1016/j.dcn.2015.11.005*

Diamond, A., & Ling, D. S. (2019). Aerobic-exercise and resistance-training interventions have been among the least effective ways to improve executive functions of any method tried thus far. *Developmental Cognitive Neuroscience, 37,* 100572. *https://doi.org/10.1016/j.dcn.2018.05.001*

Doebel, S. (2020). Rethinking executive function and its development. *Perspectives on Psychological Science, 15*(4), 942–956. *https://doi.org/10.1177/1745691620904771*

Dweck, C. (2006). *Mindset: The new psychology of success.* Ballantine Books.

Eccles, J. S., Midgley, C., Wigfield, A., Buchanan, C. M., Reuman, D., Flanagan, C., & Mac Iver, D. (1997). Development during adolescence: The impact of stage–environment fit on young adolescents' experiences in schools and in families (1993). In J. M. Notterman (Ed.), *The evolution of psychology: Fifty years of the American Psychologist* (pp. 475–501). American Psychological Association. *https://doi.org/10.1037/10254-034*

Fischer, K. W., & Rose, S. P. (1994). Dynamic development of coordination of components in brain and behavior: A framework for theory and research. In G. Dawson & K. W. Fischer (Eds.), *Human behavior and the developing brain* (pp. 3–66). Guilford Press.

Fischer, K. W., Rotenberg, E. J., Bullock, D. H., & Raya, P. (1993). The dynamics of competence: How context contributes directly to skill. In R. H. Wozniak & K. W. Fischer (Eds.), *Development in context: Acting and thinking in specific environments* (pp. 93–117). Lawrence Erlbaum Associates, Inc.

Fitzpatrick, C., McKinnon, R. D., Blair, C. B., & Willoughby, M. T. (2014). Do preschool executive function skills explain the school readiness gap between advantaged and disadvantaged children? *Learning and Instruction, 30*, 25–31. https://doi.org/10.1016/j.learninstruc.2013.11.003

Gioia, G. A., Isquith, P. K., Guy, S. C., & Kenworthy, L. (2015). *BRIEF-2: Behavior rating inventory of executive function: Professional manual*. Psychological Assessment Resources.

Hale, L., Kirschen, G. W., LeBourgeois, M. K., Gradisar, M., Garrison, M. M., Montgomery-Downs, H., Kirschen, H., McHale, S. M., Chang, A. M., & Buxton, O. M. (2018). Youth screen media habits and sleep: Sleep-friendly screen behavior recommendations for clinicians, educators, and parents. *Child and Adolescent Psychiatric Clinics of North America, 27*(2), 229–245. https://doi.org/10.1016/j.chc.2017.11.014

Hardiman, M., Rinne, L., & Yarmolinskaya, J. (2014). The effects of arts integration on long-term retention of academic content. *Mind, Brain, and Education, 8*(3), 144–148. https://doi.org/10.1111/mbe.12053

Keenan, L., Conroy, S., O'Sullivan, A., & Downes, M. (2019). Executive functioning in the classroom: Primary school teachers' experiences of neuropsychological issues and reports. *Teaching and Teacher Education, 86*, 102912. https://doi.org/10.1016/j.tate.2019.102912

Kolb, B., & Whishaw, I. Q. (2021). *Fundamentals of human neuropsychology*. (8th ed.). Macmillan.

Korkman, M., Lahti-Nuuttila, P., Laasonen, M., Kemp, S. L., & Holdnack, J. (2013). Neurocognitive development in 5- to 16-year-old North American children: A cross-sectional study. *Child Neuropsychology, 19*(5), 516–539. https://doi.org/10.1080/09297049.2012.705822

Leyland, A., Emerson, L. M., & Rowse, G. (2018). Testing for an effect of a mindfulness induction on child executive functions. *Mindfulness, 9*, 1807–1815. https://doi.org/10.1007/s12671-018-0923-2

Loe, I. M., Adams, J. N., & Feldman, H. M. (2019). Executive function in relation to white matter in preterm and full term children. *Frontiers in Pediatrics, 6*, 418. https://doi.org/10.3389/fped.2018.00418

Meyer, A., Rose, D. H., & Gordon, D. (2014). *Universal design for learning: Theory and practice*. CAST Professional Publishing.

Nigg, J. T. (2017). Annual Research Review: On the relations among self-regulation, self-control, executive functioning, effortful control, cognitive control, impulsivity, risk-taking, and inhibition for developmental psychopathology. *Journal of Child Psychology and Psychiatry, 58*(4), 361–383. https://doi.org/10.1111/jcpp.12675

O'Donnell Wicklund Pigozzi and Peterson Architects Inc VS Furniture & Bruce Mau Design. (2010). *The third teacher: 79 ways you can use design to transform teaching & learning.* Abrams.

Olson, K. (2009). *Wounded by school.* Teachers College Press.

Paus, T. (2005). Mapping brain maturation and cognitive development during adolescence. *Trends in Cognitive Sciences, 9*(2), 60–68. https://doi.org/10.1016/j.tics.2004.12.008

Perone, S., Simmering, V. R., & Buss, A. T. (2021). A dynamical reconceptualization of executive-function development. *Perspectives on Psychological Science, 16*(6), 1198–1208. https://doi.org/10.1177/1745691620966792

Rinne, L., Gregory, E., Yarmolinskaya, J., & Hardiman, M. (2011). Why arts integration improves long-term retention of content. *Mind, Brain, and Education, 5*(2), 89–96. https://doi.org/10.1111/j.1751-228X.2011.01114.x

Schlechty, P. C. (2011). *Engaging students: The next level of working on the work* (2nd ed.). Jossey-Bass.

Spencer, John. (2018, August 13). *Five ways to boost metacognition in the classroom.* https://spencerauthor.com/metacognition/

Sweller, J. (2011). Cognitive load theory. In J. P. Mestre & B. H. Ross (Eds.), *The psychology of learning and motivation: Cognition in education* (pp. 37–76). Elsevier Academic Press. https://doi.org/10.1016/B978-0-12-387691-1.00002-8

Verburgh, L., Königs, M., Scherder, E. J., & Oosterlaan, J. (2014). Physical exercise and executive functions in preadolescent children, adolescents and young adults: a meta-analysis. *British Journal of Sports Medicine, 48*(12), 973–979. https://doi.org/10.1136/bjsports-2012-091441

Vygotsky, L. S. (1978). *Mind in society: Development of higher psychological processes* (M. Cole, V. Jolm-Steiner, S. Scribner, & E. Souberman, Eds.). Harvard University Press. https://doi.org/10.2307/j.ctvjf9vz4

Zenner, C., Herrnleben-Kurz, S., & Walach, H. (2014). Mindfulness-based interventions in schools—a systematic review and meta-analysis. *Frontiers in Psychology, 5*, 603. https://doi.org/10.3389/fpsyg.2014.00603

Notes From the Authors

I have wanted to be a writer since I can remember. At first I thought of myself as a poet, and later a potential novelist. In college I thought very seriously about becoming a historian. Had you told the Lisa of 10 years ago that her first book would be about executive functioning and learning, she would have laughed and then probably asked, "What on earth is executive functioning?" When you explained that it relates to the development of the brain, she might have even recoiled. Brains? Weird. But, here we are. I went from mediocre child poet to history major to teacher to author writing about brains. It's been an interesting journey—one mostly guided by three things: 1) I have a nagging need to want to help the world be a better place; 2) I find people fascinating and human; and 3) I get bored easily. This last bit has led me to frequently say yes to opportunities that might not seem like they align with any clear career path.

After spending several years as a special education teacher in Maryland public schools, I joined a fledgling postgraduate fellowship program for experienced teachers at Kennedy Krieger Institute in Baltimore. I spent that year learning about brains, behavior, child development, and education law and policy from top faculty of Kennedy Krieger and the Johns Hopkins School of Medicine. I loved my time at the Center for Innovation and Leadership in Special Education so much that I never left. I now assist in the management of our unique teacher education program. I function as a bridge between the researchers and clinicians advancing our understanding of the vast array of neurovariablity of the developing brain and amazing educators seeking to improve teaching and learning for all students.

My decision to leave the classroom and join the fellowship program at Kennedy Krieger Institute was predicated on a love for my students and nagging thoughts that I could be serving them better if I just understood how the learning brain works. Why did a brain tumor on the left side of my student's brain impact the right side of his body? Why did a seizure disorder impact my student's working memory? Was there a relationship between ADHD and difficulty with reading? How much could my students' IQ really tell me about their capacity to learn? And why did the reading interventions I was handed not seem to work for many of my students?

I know that many teachers have similar thoughts and feelings. This might even be why you've picked up this book. As educators, we are often driven to learn so that others may learn better. My professional goal is to make it easier for hardworking teachers to learn the things that matter.

For too long the people working tirelessly to improve the lives of children have worked in silos. In working alongside clinicians and researchers at one of the top pediatric facilities in the world, I now know that the people studying brains and behavior care very deeply about the work of teachers. They want us to access the information they have to offer about how to better design learning environments, support the developing brains of students, and stop wasting time and resources on techniques that don't work.

What's more, they are eager to learn from teachers. There is desire for two-way communication. Books aren't a great means for two-way communication, but it is my hope that by breaking off a small chunk of what I see as one of the most important aspects of cognitive development neurologists and neuropsychologists have to share with teachers, we can start to speak the same language. One of my hopes for this book is that it is not just a guide to student executive functioning, but a brief introduction to a transdiciplinary work that needs your voice.

—LISA CAREY

***

My journey into the world of education was likely a path paved well before I could even speak. The name Alexis is derived from the Greek *Alexo,* which means "helper" or "defender." My parents must have had a sense of the purpose I was supposed to serve in this world. In fact, my mother has guided me to activate my own strengths while acknowledging and improving my areas for growth throughout my life. That has ultimately guided all that I do personally and professionally. Early on, as a preschool student, I was enrolled in a Montessori school where my curiosity and agency were nurtured inside and outside the classroom. My brother and I were encouraged to question, explore, create, share, and reflect. Not only were we taught to tap into our social-emotional skills and mindfulness, but we were raised in a way that modeled and fostered just that. Before mindfulness was discussed in the mainstream media as it now is, we were raised to be present and notice what was happening both around and within us. I attribute most of who I am and how I work to the way I was raised: to learn from all that I interact with and find lessons in nature, community, family, connection, and in the simplicity of each moment. Now, I have my own meditation teacher and am trained to teach and guide others in their own awareness training. It is a privilege to learn and grow personally as I support and facilitate learning with and for others. I am grateful to share much of what I have learned through my personal experiences and lessons, coupled with years of training and working with amazing colleagues, mentors, research teams, educators, families, and—most importantly—learners of all ages.

In reflecting on my own journey to get to this point, I recognize that my purpose has always been rooted in learning and improving systems to better support others. In high school I was drawn to community service, peer counseling, and working with school administrators to improve our school community for all learners. I've always had a passion for fairness and helping others. Even though my original major in college was broadcast journalism, I was drawn to the field of education. The skills I acquired in my studies and internships for broadcast journalism led me to work with expert sports broadcasters, serve as one of the founders of the Greyhound Network at Loyola University in Baltimore, and study with incredible professors both in the US and abroad, who helped me hone my voice and research skills while utilizing technical skills to best deliver an impactful production. All of this certainly contributed to my roles inside and outside the classroom teaching students, educators, caregivers, and administrators alike. During my undergraduate studies, I continued with my leadership and broadcasting interests while making the official switch to study education as my primary focus.

In my first teaching placement (the first semester I declared education as my major at Loyola), I worked with the dedicated staff at the Forbush School in the Sheppard Pratt system. This experience matched me with learners who were experiencing complex challenges that required a unique approach to teaching and learning. I have taken this experience with me in every learning environment I've ever entered, as well as a deep appreciation of the variability among all learners and the support systems around them. Following my undergraduate studies, I ended up expanding my horizons in New Jersey across the fields of education and psychology. Once I arrived for my graduate training, I quickly learned that my personal philosophy about education, which was also influenced by dedicated mentors, classmates, colleagues, and the work I had been doing, had a name: Universal Design for Learning (UDL).

While studying applied developmental and educational psychology at Boston College, I knew that stronger bridges needed to be built from research to practice. Though my training at Loyola had been systems based and focused on the whole child, many of the interventions we learned were based on a more prescriptive model. While my mentors and I integrated many supports into the learning environments I worked at in Baltimore, I always knew that we needed to do more. Rather than just reacting or responding to challenges that arise in learning environments, I dedicated my work to empowering learners, educators, and families to better understand development from a systems theory approach in terms of neurodiversity, emotion, and cognition. Following the completion of my graduate work, I shifted back into the classroom while also working on research teams and professional development trainings with CAST, and later as a part of their UDL Cadre to empower educational systems to think differently about teaching and learning.

My current position as the founder and owner of Reid Connect, LLC, is focused on helping disengaged learners find their way back to a purposeful path in their lives and learning. My work traverses psychoeducation around neurodiversity, how affect and emotion impact executive functioning skills, task initiation, motivation, and other related behaviors. In collaboration with other therapists, I work to determine what barriers get in learners' way and shape an approach that best meets their needs. Through our work together, learners and their support systems (families, educators, etc.) recognize their strengths while bolstering areas for growth by increasing strategic thinking and learning. These skills and strategies are established and practiced to better navigate challenges while increasing mindfulness, awareness, and more balanced emotional health.

In my work with clients, the focus is on executive functioning skill development and how to build more strategic learning skills, but it is not bound only to traditional learning environments. This work is fostered through all areas of life, beyond the classroom and into real-life situations. Each individual I work with develops skills that allow them to autonomously navigate most situations in a planful, intentional, and strategic way. I work to meet each individual where they are, often sharing the role of their prefrontal cortex to strategize, model, and reflect with them through challenges to get started, while supporting them to rewrite the narratives they have about learning or tasks being "too hard" or their skills not being "good enough."

With the advent of Amazon Alexa, Apple watches, and other technological gadgets, there are many ways to scaffold planning, organization, and time management, though these tools do not replace building and improving skills. I sometimes joke with the adolescent learners I work with that my name is "Alexis, not Alexa," as they frequently ask for reminders and information to help them along their learning path. My goal is for them to eventually taper their sessions with me and tell me "I've got this"—ultimately, not needing our meetings or my support because they've established habits that support them across contexts, and can monitor and regulate their emotions to traverse different scenarios and challenges that may arise. Technology has given us nearly limitless access to information while also leaving society reliant on it. My role as a guide, coach, or confidante is to help everyone I work with build skills that ultimately lead to strong, secure, connected, autonomous, and purposeful lives. When they understand, practice, and are aware of their own strategic learning skills, so too do they find their independence and confidence. This is our intention for this book, too.

In 2022, in the wake of a global pandemic, I joined forces with my brother and colleague, Dr. Gerald Reid (a clinical and sport psychologist and neuropsychological evaluator), to create and broadcast the Reid Connect-ED podcast. This is our way to share the knowledge and wisdom we have accrued over time as well as the brilliant work of many colleagues and friends in our respective fields. As you might imagine, we integrate discussions through the lens of learning, executive functioning, and mental health through all the topics we discuss and aim to ED-ucate listeners on topics that may benefit their lives. Sharing information that many may not have access to or know about will hopefully break down some of the stigma around struggles across different areas of life. The Reid Connect-ED podcast can be found wherever you stream your favorite podcasts or at *https://reidconnect.com/reid-connect-ed-podcast*.

Despite having years of training from exceptional institutions, neither Lisa nor I were explicitly taught as educators to support, scaffold, and help train executive functioning skills as we have defined them here in this book in our classrooms. Though the educational landscape is shifting to incorporate more educational neuroscience and developmental psychology into teacher training and professional development, there is still more work to be done. We challenge you to think not about the deficits that exist in the work you do, but about how small shifts in your approach or more explicit proactive planning can better support executive functioning for all learners in your learning environments.

Through our own teaching and learning experiences, we have researched, studied, supported, and helped train learners of all ages to best support executive functions as a foundation for building expert learning skills. We hope that this book will serve as a primer for teachers in training and experts alike to expand upon a repertoire of strategies to include executive functioning skills through the UDL framework to best meet the needs of all learners. We believe that appropriate support for executive functioning skills across development not only will lead to more confident, strategic, and complex thinking and learning but also help nurture future generations in and out of the classroom. Thank you for coming along on this journey with us as we aim to reach and teach educators around the world about the importance of understanding executive functioning in practice across development.

As you navigate through this book, we want you to remember that to improve executive functioning skills for learners around you, it's just as important to support your own executive functioning skills. On the website *https://publishing.cast.org/supplemental/executive-functioning-in-students-additional-resources* we have provided tools you can use for points of reflection to determine what you need to find and maintain balance in your life as a professional and person. Those in the helping professions—educators, healers, and the like—tend to do more for others than we do for ourselves. This is an important notion to remember so that what we do for others doesn't compete with what we do for ourselves. When our plates are overflowing and we become emotional or feel residual stress or challenge from all that's going on in our lives, our own executive functioning skills become vulnerable. Especially during this time of complexity, as the many layers of our societal and educational systems are shifting and changing each day, we hope you can find solace in strategies and patience for your situation as you work to support all of those in your learning environment.

One of the greatest supports we can provide to ourselves and our learners is compassion for the facts that we are all learning and improving, that each new point or strategy we learn or improve is a process, that we all need supports or scaffolds at different points of our development. We are all in this together and hope that this book provides insight and guidance that brings clarity and compassion for the great work you do for your learners each day.

—ALEXIS REID

Acknowledgments

There is a long list of women who supported and guided me on this journey. Dr. Martha Denckla spent her time teaching me and other educators about neurodevelopment and executive functions and stressed the importance of being a strong science communicator. Dr. Lisa Jacobson pushed (and still pushes) my thinking and learning about neurodevelopment, executive functions, research methods, and programming to support kids. Dr. Alison Pritchard supported my goal of becoming a researcher. Dr. Liz Berquist started me on my UDL journey and popped in and out of my life just when I needed her, like a UDL fairy godmother. And educators Nicole Norris and Emily Caster taught me to be a better teacher, pushed me to think about systematic changes in practical ways, and always have modeled excellent decision-making.

—LISA CAREY

I have been mentored, guided, and taught by incredible educators over the course of my training and career. Thanks to mentors and professors at both Loyola University in Maryland and Boston College, I have been blessed to explore the many facets of education, learning, cognitive and neurosciences, and educational and developmental psychology. In professional circles, I have learned from and created programming and resources with incredible colleagues who are now friends across both the mental health and educational fields in the US and around the world. Each professor, teacher, classmate, colleague, school system, and student I have encountered has played a role in my work and life—most especially, my brother, colleague, podcast co-host, co-author, and best friend, Dr. Gerald Reid.

—ALEXIS REID

Index

A

A Taxonomy for Teaching, Learning, and Assessment, 100
ability, 37, 38
academic outcomes, 25
action and expression
    multiple means for, 81
    overview of, 48–50
    self-regulation and, 52
ADHD, 38, 42
adolescence, 40–43, 97
adulthood, early, 43–45
affective network, 48, 51, 53
age
    and breaks in instruction, 18, 36–37
    and cognitive flexibility, 30, 31
    and executive functioning, 34–45, 54
    and inhibitory control, 28
    learning environment and, 59
    and task complexity, 16
agendas/schedules, 87, 90–92, 131–133
agreements, 115, 117–120
all-or-nothing mentality, 62, 63, 68, 72, 109
alternates, 62
anxiety
    and scheduling changes, 138
    and test-taking, 29
    and working memory, 89
    See also stress
apprenticeship, cognitive, 153–154
articulation, 19, 154
arts, the, 157–158
avoidance, 98
awareness, 155

B

backward planning, 72
balance, 53, 141
basal ganglia, 33
behavior
    brain and, 50
    calling out, 98
    and engagement spectrum, 116
    of executive dysfunction, 14, 15–18
    goal-directed, 30–31
    inhibitory control and, 38, 39
    managing impulsive, 125
    self-evaluation of, 139–141
    shifts in, 99
    and skill development, 118–119
Bloom, Benjamin, 100
Bloom's taxonomy, 100
body, the, 16, 53, 158
Boston College, 2
brain, the
    brain/body links, 158
    executive functions in, 33–46, 52–54
    learning and, 2, 48, 50
    and mindfulness, 156
    networks in, 48, 51

brain, the (*continued*)
    variability in, 45
    video games and, 124
    See also neurodevelopment
brainstorming, 74
breaks, 138–145
breath, 54, 141, 144, 146, 154, 156–157

C

calm, 25, 138, 154
Carey, Lisa, 1–2
CAST, 2
cerebellum, 33
challenges
    challenge/support balance, 53
    cognitive demands of, 23–24
    cognitive flexibility amidst, 99
    developmentally-appropriate, 36
    non-academic, 40–41
    pauses during, 105
    skills to tackle, 4
    SMART goal system, 73
    timing of, 146–147
    of "why," 102
changes, 132, 135
checklists, 91–92, 130, 131
checkpoints, 64, 68, 70, 81, 83, 108, 134
childhood, early, 35–37, 136
chunking information, 90, 92–93, 146
City Neighbors Charter School, 20
clutter, 121
coaching, 154
Cogmed, 153
cognitive apprenticeship, 153–154
cognitive dissonance, 115
cognitive function, 2, 18
cognitive load, 86
cognitive thinking traps, 62
collaboration, 88, 117–120
college students
    executive function in, 42
    neurodevelopment for, 43–45
    time management by, 44

commitment, 116
community, classroom, 115, 117, 118, 119
compassion, 45, 138
completing tasks, 16–17
completion, defining, 82–85
complex tasks, 16
conferencing
    meaningful discussion questions, 104
    and metacognition cycle, 101
    about scheduling, 146
    for self-reflection, 98
    student-led, 109
context demands
    ADD and, 42–43
    in high school, 42
    in middle school, 40–41
    perspective and, 100
    and taking breaks, 139
cortical thickness, 37
Covey, Stephen, 93
creativity, 72
curiosity, 70, 72, 74, 108, 124

D

Dash, Megan, 20
deadlines, 12, 81
decision-making skills, 68
defensiveness, 62
demands, cognitive, 24
Denckla, Dr. Martha, 45, 152
developmental disabilities
    and communication, 19
    and executive function difference, 38
    support for, 43
Diamond, Dr. Adele, 18, 152
digital tools, 122–127, 133
directions, following, 16
discipline, 158
discussions, meaningful, 104
disorganization, 12–13
distractions/distractibility

and inhibitory control, 15–16
minimizing, 121–122
and overwhelm, 146
and scheduling, 132
stress and, 85–86
of technology, 123, 125
and time monitoring, 133
Dweck, Carol, 69
dyslexia, 12
dysregulation, 40, 141

E

early childhood, 35–37, 136
editing, 99–100
elementary school, 34–40, 97
emotions
    agreements/discussion about, 119
    emotional self-regulation, 51, 53
    emotional stressors, 53, 54
    influence on cognitive skills, 64
    and mindfulness, 155
    predictability and, 131
    and prioritizing tasks, 80
    and taking breaks, 139
empathy, 20, 162
empowerment, 162
engagement
    and cognitive load, 86
    collaboration about, 117
    joyful, 152
    overview of, 48–50
    self-assessment of, 120
    self-regulation and, 52
    spectrum of, 115–116
entertainment, 123–124
environment. *See* learning environment
Evidence for ESSA, 152
executive dysfunctions
    behavioral indicators of, 14, 15–18
    defined, 13–14
    learner knowledge of, 19–20
    and learning environment, 13–14, 18–19
    usefulness of understanding, 20–21
executive functions
    and academic outcomes, 25
    age and, 26, 34–37
    arts and music for, 157–158
    and the brain, 50
    via cognitive apprenticeship, 153–154
    and dysfunction, 13–21
    for engagement, 117
    in everyday life, 25, 152
    exercise and, 158–160
    foundational, 15, 28
    for goal-directed learning, 30–31, 62–65
    introduction to, 114
    and learning environment, 34, 35, 113–114
    lifelong skill development in, 3, 4
    list of core, 26–32
    long-lasting benefits of, 151
    metacognition for, 97
    via mindfulness, 154–157
    and neurodevelopment, 33–46
    for novel situations, 23–24, 25
    pruning for optimized, 40
    and self-regulation, 50–52
    struggling with, 11–12
    supportive scaffolds for, 6, 58–60
    teacher familiarity with, 1–2, 161
    UDL framework for, 50
    variability in, 38, 45, 52–54
exercise, 158–159
expectations
    clearly defined, 82–85, 132, 137
    creating classroom, 115
    developmentally appropriate, 38, 44
    non-academic, 40–41
    periodic review of, 119
    reminders about, 130, 138
experience
    and brain development, 45

experience (*continued*)
    and executive functioning, 53
    perspective and, 100
explicit examples, 73, 102

F

familiarity, 23–24
fear, 62, 65
feedback
    encouraging self-reflection and, 68–70
    and metacognition cycle, 101
    as modeled by teachers, 108
    by peers, 106–107
    specificity of, 102
    supports for, 59
    timely and positive, 102, 105–106, 109–110
fidgets, 125
"finished," defining, 82–85
flexibility, cognitive
    and activity transitions, 17
    and brain development, 34
    and break taking, 141
    with challenges, 25, 99
    deficits in, 19, 32
    feedback for, 105
    and metacognition, 98–99
    overview of, 30–32
    and play, 30, 31
    primary function of, 107
    and reciprocal teaching, 153
    via self-assessment, 68
    supports for, 19
    in young children, 36
focus
    and break taking, 144
    and cognitive flexibility, 30
    via fidgets, 125
    and inhibitory control, 139
    and prioritizing tasks, 84
following directions, 16
freedom, 43
frontal lobe, 33, 38, 50, 53

G

games
    go/no-go games, 27–28, 37
    time management as, 148
    video games, 124
generalizability, 152
genetics, 45
goal-directed behavior
    and cognitive flexibility, 30
    and executive functioning, 51
goals
    balance in, 141–142
    checklists for, 136
    creating clear, 62–65, 69
    defining expectations, 82–85
    feedback on, 68–70
    flexibility in achieving, 61
    long-term vs. short-term, 86–87
    planning phase, 67–68, 89
    SMART goals, 70–77
    starting, 62, 63, 66–67
    supports for, 59
go/no-go games, 27–28, 37
gray matter, 38
group assignments, 31
growth, bodily, 39
growth mindset, 69
guidebooks, journals as, 110
guiding questions, 102–105, 153

H

habits, 64, 124
health, 154
help, 144
high school, 41–43
highlighting important points, 93
hormones, 40
hyperactive ADD, 42

I

IEP (individualized educational plan), 12, 43
illness, 53, 54

impulsivity, 15, 27–28
inattentive ADD, 42
independence
    in adolescence, 41
    in early adulthood, 43
    and effective transitions, 136
    via familiarity with rules, 60
    vs. reassurance seeking, 65
    in reflection, 106–107
inflexibility, cognitive, 63, 68, 98
inhibitory control
    and activity transitions, 17
    balance in, 115
    and brain development, 34
    and exercise, 158
    as foundational, 15, 28, 37
    and frustrations, 12–13
    games to develop, 27–28
    lack of, 15, 139
    and misbehavior, 39
    overview of, 27–28
    and prioritizing tasks, 79–80
    in young children, 36
initiating tasks, 66–67
instructions
    clear and variable, 18
    working memory and, 29
intentionality, 141
interactivity
    in Bloom's taxonomy, 100
    of brain function, 34
    of cognitive skills, 26
    executive function/self-regulation, 51
interruptions, 23–24

J

Jacobson, Dr. Lisa, 34
journaling, 110
joy, 152
junior high, 40

K

K–12 learning, 5–6, 34–43

Keenan, Dr. Lisa, 11
Kennedy Krieger Institute, 1
kindergarten, 34–37
knowledge
    activating prior, 74
    to appropriately guide students, 39
    and executive functioning, 39
    highlighting critical, 93
    retaining, 89
    for task completion, 16

L

learners
    access to supports, 60
    giving/receiving of feedback, 107
    meaningful discussions with, 104
    reassurance seeking by, 65
    and reciprocal teaching, 153
    self-care for, 142
    strategic, 71
    understanding of dysfunctions, 19–20
    uniqueness of, 4–5, 53
    unmet needs of, 14
learning
    Bloom's taxonomy of, 100
    and brain development, 1–2, 34–45
    supporting process of, 59
    via technology, 123
    UDL framework for, 48–50
    varying engagement with, 116–117
learning environment
    and the brain, 34, 45, 52–54
    classroom climate, 114–117
    collaborative work agreements, 117–120
    defined, 58–59
    and executive dysfunction, 13–14, 18–19
    executive functions and, 2, 25, 34, 162
    flexibility in, 5, 21
    gaps in, 21
    influence of, 35, 113–114

learning environment (*continued*)
   and inhibitory control, 28
   intentionality in, 70
   mindfulness in, 159–160
   minimizing distractions in, 121–122
   overwhelm in, 86
   routine in, 130
   sensory stimuli in, 16
   simplifying systems in, 6
   struggles and, 38–39
   technology in, 122–127
   uniqueness of, 4–5
LEGO bricks, 31
limbic system, 33, 53
Loyola University in Baltimore, 2

M

mastery, demonstrating, 29, 91
medical treatment, 54
memory, working. *See* working memory
mentors, 44, 153, 154
metacognition
   antithesis of, 98
   Bloom's taxonomy and, 100–101
   cycle of, 101
   and exercise, 158
   guiding questions for, 102–105
   and learner variability, 99–101
   self-reflection and, 97–99
middle childhood, 37–40
middle school, 40, 97
mindfulness, 138, 154–157
mindsets
   all-or-nothing mentality, 62, 63, 68, 72
   fixed vs. growth, 69
   process mindset, 67–68, 69, 71
mistakes, 65
modeling by teachers, 105, 154
monitoring time, 133–135, 146
motivation, 42

movement breaks, 37
multitasking, 28, 86
music, 157–158
myelination, 38, 41

N

needs, unmet, 14
negative feedback, 109
neurodevelopment
   adolescence, 41–43
   early adolescence, 40–41
   early adulthood, 43–45
   early childhood, 34–37
   instructional links with, 47
   and learning environment, 54
   middle childhood, 37–40
   as nonlinear, 36
   pruning in, 40
   variability in, 45, 52–54
neuropsychology, developmental, 26, 50
"normal," 35
novel situations, 23–24

O

options
   to reach goals, 67
   too many, 63, 86
   See also variability
organization
   agenda/schedule for, 87, 90
   and clear goals, 69
   for college students, 44–45
   and developmental disability, 12
   supports for, 59
   with too many options, 63
overwhelm, 139, 146

P

patience
   with frustrations, 25
   with middle school students, 40
   with prioritizing tasks, 80

self-regulatory skills for, 138
with young adults, 44
patterns of thought, shifting, 17–18
pauses, 138–145
peer feedback, 106–107
Pendred, Tracy, 20
perfectionism, 63–64, 65
physical activity, 158–160
pivoting, 30
planning phase, 67–68, 72, 82, 84
points, awarding, 67, 71
pomodoro sessions, 140, 146
positive feedback, 105–106, 109
practice, intentional, 58, 130
predictability, 129–131, 136
prefrontal cortex, 33, 34
prioritizing tasks
    and assignment overload, 86
    and balance, 141–142
    collaboration for, 88
    creating a plan for, 89–95
    defining "finished," 82–85
    importance of, 79–80
    priorities matrix, 93–94
    reflection on, 147
    schedule for, 87
    supports for, 80–82
    and working memory, 85–88
    and wrapping up work, 136
problem-solving, 30, 31, 42, 123, 162, 163
process
    agreements about, 118
    discussed with students, 75
    evaluating your, 98
    focus on, 84
    goals and, 69, 73
    planning as part of, 89–90
    and prioritizing tasks, 82
    process mindset, 67–68, 71
procrastination, 62, 64, 121
programmed cell death, 40
pruning, 40

punishment
    curiosity vs., 69–70
    vs. skill development, 39, 118

Q
questions, guiding, 102–105, 153

R
reassurance seeking, 65
reciprocal teaching, 152–153
recognition network, 48
reflection
    activating, 105
    in cognitive apprenticeship, 154
    on engagement, 117
    independent, 106–107
    via journaling, 110
    metacognition and, 97
    mindfulness and, 156
    on needs for success, 147
    self-reflection, 68–70, 98, 107–109
    about technology, 125
    See also feedback
Reid, Alexis, 2–3
Reid, Dr. Gerald, 109
ReidConnect-ED podcast, 109
relaxation, 154, 156
reminders, 12, 130, 134, 138
representation
    multiple modalities for, 91
    overview of, 48–50
    self-regulation and, 52
resilience, 99
responsibility
    clearly defining, 137
    mentors to serve, 44
    reminders about, 130–131
    with technology, 122
retaining information, 89
routines
    vs. learning new things, 25
    setting agendas, 131–133

routines (*continued*)
    stress of changed, 23–24
    support via, 129–131
    time monitoring, 133–135
rubrics
    engagement self-assessment, 120
    for goal criteria, 67, 68
    sample, 83
    to set priorities, 81–82
rules, class, 115

S

scaffolding, 154
scheduling
    including breaks in, 145
    for organization, 90–92
    for prioritizing tasks, 87
    setting agendas, 131–133
    of transitions, 135–138
Schlechty, Dr. Phillip, 115
Schlechty's Levels of Engagement model, 115–116, 119
school year, 135
self-advocacy, 20
self-assessment
    of behaviors, 139–141
    of engagement, 120
    of process/skills, 98
self-care, 142, 162
self-reflection, 68–70, 98, 107–109
self-regulation, 50–52, 53, 138, 155
sensory stimuli, 16, 37, 122, 126, 156
Seven Habits of Highly Productive People, 93
shame, 98
sharing, 88
shifting/pivoting, 17–18, 30
Simon Says, 27–28, 37
skills
    age and complexity of, 16
    as context dependent, 13
    prioritizing practice of, 84
    self-assessment of, 98

skills, cognitive
    decision-making, 68
    in everyday life, 152
    executive functions as, 3, 4, 11, 14, 23, 26
    gaps in, 20–21
    higher-order, 153
    independent use of, 60, 65
    interactive nature of, 26
    masking skill gaps, 42–43
    mindfulness, 154–155
    support for, 58–60
    of young adults, 44
SMART goals, 70–77
social dynamics, 42, 44
space, clearing, 121, 126, 132
speaking out, 15, 27
Spears, Kimberly, 20
stage-environment fit, 54
starting, 62, 63, 66–67
stoplights, 27
strategic network, 48, 50, 51, 53, 73
strategic thinking, 30, 66, 99
strengths
    highlighting, 106
    masking skill gaps with, 42–43
    praising learner, 109
stress
    and clear goals, 63
    and distraction, 86
    effect on executive functions, 53
    in learning environment, 18
    and non-academic expectations, 40–41
    and procrastination, 64
    about schedule changes, 132, 138
    and test-taking, 29
    and working memory, 89
structure, order and, 130
struggles
    appropriate assistance for, 38–40
    destigmatizing, 19
    with executive functions, 11–12

with prioritizing tasks, 80, 86
understanding learner, 20–21
with "why," 102
"stuck" points
   all-or-nothing mentality about, 62
   identifying, 17
   keeping track of, 110
   triggered by stress/struggle, 99
success, 118, 147
support
   balanced with challenge, 53
   for executive functioning, 58–60, 162
   lack of teacher, 69–70
   via learning environment, 114
   offering explicit, 108
   predictability/routine as, 130
   for self-regulation, 51
   for setting priorities, 80–82
   for transitions, 135–138

T

task completion
   behaviors prohibiting, 27
   checklists for, 136
   dysfunctional, 16–17
   executive functions for, 63
   as a game, 148
   needs for successful, 147
   See also prioritizing tasks
teachers
   acceptance of variability by, 45
   community of, 163
   executive function education for, 1–2, 161
   modeling best practices by, 105, 123
   reassurance seeking with, 65
   teachable moments, 69–70
   technology use by, 123
   vulnerability with students, 77
teaching
   via feedback, 105–106

as push into the unfamiliar, 25
reciprocal teaching, 152–153
UDL framework for, 48–50
technology, 122–127
test-taking, 29
think-alouds, 102–105
The Third Teacher, 113
thought
   all-or-nothing mentality, 63
   disorganized, 16
   effortful, 23–24
   flexible. *See* flexibility, cognitive
   shifting patterns of, 17–18
   thinking aloud, 103
time management
   breaks in, 143
   for college-age learners, 44
   as a game, 148
   in planning for goals, 73
   and prioritizing tasks, 81, 93–94
   for SMART goals, 77
time monitoring, 133–135, 145
to-do lists, 95
tools, evaluating, 126–127
transitions between activities, 17, 135–138
translational bridges, 47
Triple A exercise, 144–145
trust, 70, 130
typing vs. writing, 99–100

U

UDL (Universal Design for Learning) Guidelines
   and brain function, 33, 51
   on executive function, 1, 4, 5, 50–52
   framework overview, 48–50
   on goals, 66
   on learner variability, 4
   learning barriers and, 14
   and learning environment, 52–54
   and neurovariability, 52–54

UDL Guidelines (*continued*)
    precursors of, 100
    and self-regulation, 50–52
    technology and, 122
    tools supporting, 58, 59, 60
uncertainty, 132, 135
undergraduate students, 42
unfamiliarity
    cognitive demands of, 23
    and flexible thought, 30
    and new goals, 61
    teaching as encounter with, 25
    and working memory, 28–29
uniqueness, learner, 4–5
urgencies, prioritizing, 93–94

V

validation, 119
Vanderbilt University, 41
variability
    and brain development, 35
    in executive functions, 52–54
    in information delivery, 90–91
    in learning engagement, 116–117
    and learning supports, 59
    in modes of instruction, 18
    neurovariability, 45, 52–54
    too many options, 63
variability, learner
    and clear goals, 63
    and distractibility, 122
    importance of recognizing, 5
    and metacognition, 99–101
    supports for, 43
    technology and, 122
verbal cues, missed, 16
video games, 124
virtual learning, 16

vulnerability, 77, 105, 162

W

wellness, 154
What Works Clearinghouse, 152
white matter, 38, 41
"why"
    of class rules, 115
    explicitness about, 102
    feedback revealing the, 105
    sharing goals and, 73
working memory
    and activity transitions, 17
    and brain development, 34
    overview of, 28–30
    prioritization and, 85–88
    reducing load for, 19
    strengthening skills in, 89–95
    supports for, 13, 19
    in young children, 36
"wrapping up" work, 136
writing, feedback on, 105

Y

Yale Center for Emotional
    Intelligence, 119
young learners
    barriers to learning for, 36
    brain development in, 34–37
    cognitive flexibility in, 30
    executive functions and the
        brain, 33
    movement breaks for, 37
    time demands for, 18, 36

Z

Zone of Proximal Development
    (ZPD), 53

About the Authors

Dr. Lisa Beth Carey is a teacher educator and researcher with a focus on improving educational experiences and outcomes for students with neurodevelopmental disabilities. Dr. Carey was one of the inaugural fellows of the Center for Innovation and Leadership in Special Education, where she received extensive training in the cognitive neuroscience of learning, behavioral science, school law, and research methods.

Before she was accepted as one of the inaugural fellows at the Center for Innovation and Leadership in Special Education, Dr. Carey was a special educator in St. Mary's and Baltimore Counties of Maryland, specializing in inclusive practices for students with emotional-behavioral and developmental disabilities. She has taught as adjunct special education faculty at St. Mary's College of Maryland and Towson University. Dr. Carey is a member of the CAST National Faculty and has facilitated Universal Design for Learning (UDL) professional learning projects nationwide.

Dr. Carey holds a BA in history from St. Mary's College of Maryland, a MEd in Teaching from Goucher College, an Administrator One advanced certificate from Towson University, and a doctorate in Instructional Technology from Towson University.

Alexis Reid, MA, is an educational therapist and learning consultant who specializes in executive functioning (EF); social emotional learning (SEL); teaching, learning, and human development;

as well as designing flexible and accessible learning environments through Universal Design for Learning (UDL). In her private practice, Reid Connect, LLC, located in Boston, Cape Cod, and virtually, Alexis supports individuals and the systems in which they exist at the intersections of learning and well-being. Furthermore, Alexis has been a CAST UDL National Faculty and Cadre member for over a decade. She facilitates online and in-person professional development courses and trainings around the globe on UDL as well as workshops focusing on executive functioning and SEL.

Alexis and her brother, licensed psychologist Dr. Gerald Reid, PhD, are also co-hosts of the ReidConnect-Ed Podcast, which aims to connect and educate curious-minded individuals with information relating to mental health, learning, performance, education, wellness, executive functioning, and much more.

More from CAST Professional Publishing

Building Executive Function and Motivation in the Middle Grades: A Universal Design for Learning Approach

By Susanne Croasdaile

"This book reads easily in a sitting, but like the best instructional practices, can be broken into chunks so that teachers can quickly implement meaningful, research-based routines to support executive function in their classrooms. I've personally witnessed teachers using these strategies, and the difference they've made in their classrooms are remarkable."

—JEFF BOARMAN, Assistant Principal, Carter G. Woodson Middle School

ISBN 978-1-943085-00-2 (Print)
ISBN 978-1-943085-01-9 (ePub)
144 PAGES | © 2023

UDL Now! A Teacher's Guide to Applying Universal Design for Learning, Third Edition

By Katie Novak, with a foreword by George Couros

"Katie Novak's well-articulated know-how, about how to put UDL into practice, has helped many thousands of educators. . . . She can describe what she does without evaporating the awe, the joy, or the sublimity of what great teaching is really like."

—DAVID H. ROSE, co-founder of CAST

ISBN 978-1-930583-82-5 (Print)
ISBN 978-1-930583-83-2 (ePub)
ISBN 978-1-943085-24-8 (Audiobook)
196 PAGES | © 2022

Universal Design for Learning in English Language Arts

By Katie Novak, Ryan Hinkle, Brianne Parker, Jina Poirier, and Anne Wolff

Katie Novak has teamed up with four literacy experts to offer educators a practical guide to integrating Universal Design for Learning in the English language arts classroom. The book demonstrates how to build rich, collaborative, and engaging literacy environments for students with varied backgrounds and needs.

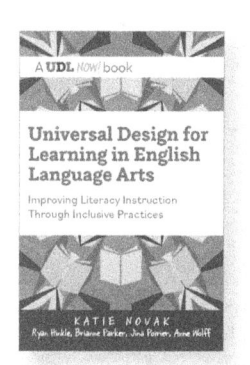

ISBN 978-1-943085-08-8 (Print)
ISBN 978-1-943085-09-5 (ePub)
184 PAGES | © 2023

For more information, visit **www.castpublishing.org** or wherever books are sold. For bulk orders, email **publishing@cast.org**.

More from CAST Professional Publishing

Elevating Co-teaching with Universal Design for Learning, Revised and Expanded Edition

By Elizabeth Stein, foreword by Marilyn Friend

"This book is an enlightening roadmap for teaching partners who are working diligently to keep their expectations high while taking into account all the different abilities their students bring to the classroom."

—MARILYN FRIEND, Professor Emerita, University of North Carolina at Greensboro

ISBN 978-1-930583-98-6 (Print)
ISBN 978-1-930583-99-3 (ePub)
242 PAGES | © 2023

Humanizing Classroom Management: Restorative Practices and Universal Design for Learning

By Elizabeth Stein

"Our schools and institutions need educators who are courageous enough to acknowledge that what we are currently doing is not meeting the needs of all learners. . . . Elizabeth Stein not only acknowledges this but provides readers with tools that are necessary to implement these practices with fidelity."

—MIRKO CHARDIN, Chief Equity and Inclusion Officer, Novak Education

ISBN 978-1-943085-20-0 (Print)
ISBN 978-1-943085-21-7 (ePub)
116 PAGES | © 2024

Transform Your Teaching with Universal Design for Learning: Six Steps to Jumpstart Your Practice

By Jennifer L. Pusateri

"Putting UDL into practice can be daunting for teachers who are just starting out. Jennifer L. Pusateri puts them at ease as she suggests step-by-step strategies to transform our teaching with this powerful framework."

—ANDRATESHA FRITZGERALD, founder of Building Blocks of Brilliance LLC

ISBN 978-1-930583-95-5 (Print)
ISBN 978-1-930583-94-8 (ePub)
224 PAGES | © 2022

For more information, visit **www.castpublishing.org** or wherever books are sold. For bulk orders, email **publishing@cast.org**.

MORE FROM ○CAST

CAST is a nonprofit education research and development organization that created the Universal Design for Learning framework and UDL Guidelines. Our mission is to transform education design and practice until learning has no limits.

CAST supports learners and educators at every level through a variety of offerings:

- Innovative professional development
- Accessibility and inclusive technology resources
- Research, design, and development of inclusive and effective solutions
- Credentials for Universal Design for Learning
- And much more

Visit www.cast.org to learn more.

○CAST | Until learning has no limits®

Printed in the USA
CPSIA information can be obtained
at www.ICGtesting.com
JSHW011154240624
65087JS00005B/10

9 781943 085187